Passover Haggadah
The Feast of Freedom

Passover Haggadah

The Feast of Freedom

הגדה
של פסח

Edited by Rachel Anne Rabinowicz

Illustrated by Dan Reisinger

The Rabbinical Assembly

Editor's Note

It has been an illuminating experience to collaborate with Rabbi Max Routtenberg, Rabbi Wolfe Kelman and Rabbi Jules Harlow—a remarkable rabbinic triumvirate. Their erudition, their sensitivity and their insights have enriched page after page of this Haggadah. Special acknowledgments are due to Rabbi Harlow for his masterly stylization of the *Arami oved avi* text, and for his luminous translations of *Birkat Hamazon, Hallel* and *Nishmat.* Special thanks are due to Rabbi Bernard Raskas for enhancing the aesthetic dimensions of the Haggadah. I am indebted to Nina Beth Cardin for the prodigious diligence and dedication she has brought to the formidable task of coordination. And, above all, I am profoundly grateful for the creative contributions of my sister, Miriam Rabinowicz, who has added immeasurably to the cadence and clarity of the text.

Preface

Mah nishtanah? Why is this Haggadah different from all other Haggadot, from the estimated 3,000 editions that have been produced during the past 500 years? This one is different primarily because it is the first that faithfully reflects Conservative ideology.

Like all the liturgical texts of Conservative Judaism, it is deeply committed to preserving the classic tradition. At the same time, we recognize that a tradition remains alive and well when it evolves and adjusts, responding to new developments and developing new dimensions. So conservation and innovation are counter-balanced in order to present, clearly and compellingly, the perennially and universally relevant themes of freedom and redemption.

Five years ago we were charged by The Rabbinical Assembly to prepare a Haggadah. After two years of preparation, we issued a preliminary edition, for the express purpose of receiving "comments, criticisms and recommendations" from those who would use and study it.

We are grateful to the hundreds of rabbis and laymen who presented their views to us. Many useful comments and suggestions were submitted. We studied them carefully, and, after earnest consideration, made extensive revisions and rearrangements of our text. Certain passages were omitted; many new ones were added.

We have paid special attention to the presentation. This volume has been greatly enriched by the unique art of Dan Reisinger and the superb craftsmanship of our designer, Bernard Klein.

Even a brief glance reveals the degree to which we are indebted to the editor of the preliminary edition, Michael Strassfeld, for his novel arrangement of the material as a pedagogic device and his skillful use of rabbinic literature. This edition includes a number of his original commentaries. We are also indebted to Rabbi Avraham Holtz and Rabbi Yochanan Muffs for their help with the style of the Hebrew texts.

We would like to express our appreciation of the supportive role played by presidents, past and present, of the Rabbinical Assembly: Rabbi Stanley Rabinowitz, under whose administration this committee was appointed; and his successors, Rabbi Saul Teplitz and Rabbi Seymour Cohen, who reappointed us and encouraged us in our work. We are equally appreciative of the wholehearted support of Rabbi Mordecai Waxman, current chairman of the Publications Committee.

The overall task of revision and rewriting was presented to Rachel

Rabinowicz who accepted our invitation to become the editor of the Haggadah of The Rabbinical Assembly. The members of the Haggadah Committee found it a great joy to work with her. Her glowing spirit and her sparkling lyrical prose illumine every page.

It is our hope and prayer that this Haggadah, by helping to enhance our celebration of Pesaḥ, will contribute to a deeper understanding and appreciation of the Jewish experience through the centuries. May it strengthen our commitment to Judaism.

The Haggadah Committee
Max J. Routtenberg, Chairman
Jules Harlow   Wolfe Kelman

Introduction

Every individual should feel as though he or she had actually been enslaved in Mitzrayim and redeemed from Mitzrayim. Therefore, each of us should speak of our own Exodus—in the language that we understand, in the context familiar to us, and with the knowledge and experience that we have acquired.

For even if we were all scholars, even if we were all sages, even if we were all endowed with great wisdom, we would still have to use the language of our day in order to understand, to relate and to explain the story of the Exodus. This Haggadah, while retaining the basic form and flavor of the traditional text, enables us to discuss the "going forth from Mitzrayim" in terms of our own lives and times.

The problems posed by the Haggadah are not purely linguistic or stylistic. Often texts are cited which seem strange and obscure to us. The challenge has been to create new interpretations, new *midrashim*, merging the old and the new into a coherent entity, a totality of character and content, a synthesis of prayer and praise, of poetry and picture and prose, a symphony of silence and song, one narrative without end, renewing itself over and again.

In a sense, the slavery and the Exodus were not one-time occurrences. They happen in every generation. Every life is a Hillel sandwich, commingling the *maror* of bondage with the *matzah* of redemption. Only for the Simple Child are slavery and freedom absolute. What is slavery? What is freedom? Are we not free? And are we not still enslaved?

At the Seder we hear these eternal questions reverberating through the ages: the sages of B'nei B'rak in discursive discussions lasting until dawn, somber celebrants in the ghetto of Prague amid the grim gathering shadow of blood libel accusations, Marranos celebrating in stealth in Spanish cellars, inmates in the Bergen-Belsen death camp lacking *matzah* but beset by *maror* in its most bitter form, dissidents immured in Siberian prisons, and Jews in the Free World reclining at ease. We tell of events that happened centuries ago, and yet we talk of today, and we dream of tomorrow. Past, present, future . . . all become one before the One God of Israel on this night of nights, this night of watching, of looking back . . . and looking forward.

Consequently, accommodating the past while adapting to the present, this Haggadah includes the following features:

a) a guide to the requisite rituals, detailing how and why each ritual is performed. This allows people with minimal Jewish background to participate fully.
b) a commentary on the text, explaining passages and provoking questions, in order to engage all the participants.
c) alternative readings to replace or to augment the text.

By design, in the interests of freedom and flexibility, more material has been presented than can be used at any one Seder, so that each gathering can create its own mood and highlight different aspects of the celebration. The text is central and traditional; the commentaries are supplementary and optional.

The festive meal is followed by a new section, another *Maggid*, marking the latest milestones in the far-flung travels of our people. Catastrophe and consolation: each generation must endure or witness this fateful yet all too familiar cycle. Both the Holocaust and the rebirth of the State of Israel are mirrored here, for they shape our own Exodus from our own Mitzrayim. The translation attempts to fuse fidelity to the Hebrew text with a felicitous English rendering. However, Hebrew phrases and expressions which have no exact equivalents have been transliterated, not translated. A telling example is the use of Mitzrayim instead of Egypt. Mitzrayim can be related to the root צר/ *tz-r*, narrow, meaning literally "from the narrows." The violent vicissitudes of history have endowed Mitzrayim with broader connotations, so that it has come to represent repression and tyranny. Mitzrayim transcends the longitudes and latitudes of geography. Mitzrayim is every place and any place in the world where people have been (or still are) persecuted.

Finally, since Jews do not pronounce the ineffable name of God, as it appears in Hebrew, but substitute Adonai ("my Lord" or "my master"), this term is used throughout.

Additions to the second edition of The Feast of Freedom reflect the informed and constructive comments received from both scholars and lay readers. Marginal notes have been added, instructions have been further clarified and the Historical Section ("In Every Generation") has been amplified.

Preparing for the Haggadah

The Seder is without parallel in its significance, its scope, its format and its objectives. This is a very specific ceremony, carefully choreographed, designed to take place in the home, designed to involve every member of the household, particularly the children, in a ritual that is in some instances thousands of years old, in rites that are rich with layer-upon-layer of meaning. The Haggadah serves as the blueprint for the Seder, and is indispensable to its proper observance.

Our ancestors prepared themselves by reading major portions of the Haggadah on the Shabbat preceding Pesaḥ (*Shabbat Hagadol*). Similarly, all the participants in the Seder would do well to become familiar with this new text since it involves modifications and variants.

Primary responsibility rests upon the leader who must make the selections and determine the pacing. Such decisions should be made in advance, bearing in mind the essential elements of the Haggadah, the time factor, and the reservation of material for the Second Seder. The essentials, in order of appearance, are:

KIDDUSH (*The First Cup*)
MAGGID (*The Narration*)
THE SECOND CUP
THE SYMBOLIC FOODS (*Matzah, Maror, Korekh, Afikomen*)
BIRKAT HAMAZON (*The Third Cup*)
HALLEL
THE FOURTH CUP

The *Maggid* section, which recounts the story of the Exodus and explains the Seder symbols, provides interesting options. The text of *Arami oved avi* ("My father was a wandering Aramean") can be read together with the suggested *midrashim* or with different interpretations. Verses from the Book of Exodus can be substituted or interwoven. And participants can add their comments on the subject matter.

The section following the meal also allows the leader to make choices. The standard *Birkat Hamazon* can be recited, or the short version. Selections can be made at will from the historical readings, *Hallel* and the songs. Whatever the components, this segment concludes with the Fourth Cup.

While the Second Seder must also include the basic elements, there is opportunity here for creative variation. It is fitting to incorpo-

rate passages which were omitted at the First Seder, and to select for discussion different aspects of such topics as slavery and freedom, the Holocaust, Israel, and the messianic hope. Relevant material can be introduced from Jewish literature. And it would be appropriate to read the lyrical Song of Songs with some of the many interpretations of this beguiling book. Thoughtful planning will make the second night a dynamic and different reenactment of the Exodus experience.

The final motif in the *Maggid* section is the concept of redemption, symbolized by the anticipated appearance of the prophet Elijah, harbinger of the Messiah. It is proposed that the Cup of Elijah become the Fifth Cup of the Seder, the Cup of Redemption, in honor of Israel, "the beginning of the flowering of our redemption."

Setting aside a small quantity of food, recite:

בָּרוּךְ אַתָּה יהוה אֱלֹהֵינוּ מֶלֶךְ הָעוֹלָם אֲשֶׁר קִדְּשָׁנוּ
בְּמִצְוֹתָיו וְצִוָּנוּ עַל מִצְוַת עֵרוּב.

בַּהֲדֵין עֵרוּבָא יְהֵא שְׁרֵא לָנָא לְמֵפָא וּלְבַשָּׁלָא
וּלְאַטְמָנָא, וּלְאַדְלָקָא שְׁרָגָא וּלְמֶעְבַּד כָּל צָרְכָּנָא
מִיּוֹמָא טָבָא לְשַׁבְּתָא, לָנוּ וּלְכָל יִשְׂרָאֵל הַדָּרִים
בָּעִיר הַזֹּאת.

Erev Pesaḥ:
The Day Before Pesaḥ

The day before Pesaḥ is the Fast of the Firstborn, a day on which we commemorate our exemption from the fate that befell the Egyptian firstborn. It is customary for firstborn Jews and their parents to attend a *siyyum*, the final study session of a rabbinic text, which is followed by a ceremonial meal (*seudat mitzvah*). Participants are exempted from fasting.

Matzah should not be eaten on the day before Pesaḥ. Some do not eat *matzah* during the preceding month, an abstention intended to enhance the taste of *matzah* at the Seder.

Eiruv Tavshilin

Since cooking is prohibited on Shabbat, what is the procedure when Shabbat follows the first two days of Pesaḥ? It is permissible to prepare meals on yom tov for consumption on yom tov, but it is permissible to prepare meals on yom tov for consumption on Shabbat *only* if preparation is symbolically started before the beginning of the festival. Thus if Pesaḥ begins on Wednesday night, the ceremony of *eiruv tavshilin* is observed on Wednesday before sunset. Simply set aside some cooked food and *matzah* for Shabbat. This permits the preparation, during Pesaḥ, of additional food for Shabbat.

Setting aside a small quantity of food, recite:

Praised are You, Adonai our God, King of the universe who has sanctified us through His commandments, commanding us concerning the *eiruv*.

By means of this *eiruv*, we and all who live in this community are permitted to bake, cook, heat food, and make the necessary preparations during yom tov for Shabbat.

God and grammar. "Praised are You." "Who has sanctified us." Why do we shift, in the space of one brief invocation, from second person to third? This syntactical deviation accurately pinpoints the mystical ambivalence of our multi-faceted consciousness of God. How we address Him hinges on how we relate to Him. Thus the two phrases, connected by the relative pronoun (who, *asher*), reflect our awareness that the God who is near and known to us is simultaneously the Supreme Being who is distant, unknown and beyond our knowing. It was perhaps the height of religious genius to knit these numinous strands into the many blessings that are uttered every day.

13

Before the search, recite:

בָּרוּךְ אַתָּה יהוה אֱלֹהֵינוּ מֶלֶךְ הָעוֹלָם אֲשֶׁר קִדְּשָׁנוּ
בְּמִצְוֹתָיו וְצִוָּנוּ עַל בְּעוּר חָמֵץ.

After the search, recite:

כָּל חֲמִירָא וַחֲמִיעָא דְּאִכָּא בִּרְשׁוּתִי, דְּלָא חֲמִיתֵּה
וּדְלָא בַעַרְתֵּה, וּדְלָא יָדַעְנָא לֵהּ, לִבְטִיל וְלֶהֱוֵי הֶפְקֵר
כְּעַפְרָא דְאַרְעָא.

Recitation of this declaration, and a similar one the following day, prevents us from violating the prohibition against ḥametz (Exodus 13:7). In the morning, after the last meal of ḥametz, leftovers are added to the crumbs gathered the previous night. These are burned or thrown out. This concludes the ritual of banishing ḥametz from our dwellings.

In the morning, recite:

כָּל חֲמִירָא וַחֲמִיעָא דְּאִכָּא בִּרְשׁוּתִי, דַּחֲמִיתֵּה וּדְלָא
חֲמִיתֵּה, דְּבַעַרְתֵּה וּדְלָא בַעַרְתֵּה, לִבְטִיל וְלֶהֱוֵי
הֶפְקֵר כְּעַפְרָא דְאַרְעָא.

The Search for Ḥametz

The Search. "No leaven shall be found in your homes" (Exodus 12:19). "No *ḥametz* shall be seen within your borders" (Exodus 13:7). The search for *ḥametz* was instituted in response to these explicit directions. The accompanying formula, retained in the original Aramaic, dates back to the Gaonic period. It first appears in the voluminous writings of the noted Talmudist Isaac ben Jacob Alfasi (1013–1103) of Fez.

Removing the ḥametz. Rabbi Israel of Ryzhin explains the *bedikat ḥametz* procedure in this way: "In the evening we search for *ḥametz*, but we do not burn it until the next day. The searching and the burning are allegories of things to come. *Galut* is the night of exile during which we allow the *ḥametz* (the less appetizing qualities of our people) to remain in the house. But when the morning of our redemption comes, those qualities will be cast into the fire of our return and completely consumed. Then the words of Isaiah will be fulfilled: 'He will swallow up death forever. Adonai will wipe away the tears from all faces'" (Isaiah 25:8).

Nullifying the ḥametz. If, in all sincerity, we attempt to conquer temptation and to cleanse our hearts of sin (*ḥametz*), we need not brood or wallow in guilt if our attempts are not entirely successful, and we cannot entirely eradicate every speck. We get credit for good intentions, for although we must strive for perfection, it is inevitably beyond the reach of mere mortals. As Rabbi Elimelekh of Lyzhensk reminds us, "Only God is perfect."

A formal search for leaven (*bedikat ḥametz*) is conducted on the night before Pesaḥ. This symbolizes the final removal of leaven (*ḥametz*) from the home. Before the search, it is customary to deposit small pieces of bread (ten pieces, according to kabbalistic lore) in strategic places so that the inspection should have a purpose. It is traditionally carried out by the light of a candle, with a feather and a wooden spoon to collect the *ḥametz*; all this is set aside until morning. If *erev Pesaḥ* occurs on Shabbat, we search for *ḥametz* on Thursday evening. Why do we use a candle? "The spirit of man is the lamp of Adonai, searching all the inward parts" (Proverbs 20:27). If we scrutinize our premises so punctiliously, how much more scrupulously should we examine the crevices and crannies of our hearts?

Before the search, recite:

Praised are You, Adonai our God, King of the universe who has sanctified us through His commandments, commanding us to remove all *ḥametz*.

After the search, recite:

All *ḥametz* in my possession which I have not seen or removed, or of which I am unaware, is hereby nullified and ownerless as the dust of the earth.

Recitation of this declaration, and a similar one the following day, prevents us from violating the prohibition against ḥametz (Exodus 13:7). In the morning, after the last meal of ḥametz, leftovers are added to the crumbs gathered the previous night. These are burned or thrown out. This concludes the ritual of banishing ḥametz from our dwellings.

In the morning, recite:

All *ḥametz* in my possession, whether I have seen it or not, whether I have removed it or not, is hereby nullified and ownerless as the dust of the earth.

יְהִי רָצוֹן מִלְּפָנֶיךָ יהוה אֱלֹהַי וֵאלֹהֵי אֲבוֹתַי שֶׁכְּשֵׁם שֶׁאֲנִי
מְבָעֵר/מְבַעֶרֶת חָמֵץ מִבֵּיתִי וּמֵרְשׁוּתִי כֵּן אֶזְכֶּה לְבָעֵר אֶת יֵצֶר
הָרַע מִלִּבִּי, וְכֵן תְּבָעֵר אֶת כָּל הָרִשְׁעָה מִן הָאָרֶץ.

Reflection:

Adonai, our God and God of our ancestors, just as I have removed all *hametz* from my home and from my ownership, so may I evict the evil inclination from my heart, and may You dislodge the evil from the earth.

The Search for the Meaning of Ḥametz

Of all the festivals of the Jewish year, Pesaḥ alone is distinguished by special dietary requirements, namely, the laws pertaining to *hametz*. During Pesaḥ, Jews are prohibited from eating or even owning *hametz*. So what is it and why is it taboo at this time? *Hametz* is defined as any mixture of flour and water that has been allowed to ferment for more than 18 minutes. The most obvious example is bread, but grain ingredients, i.e., traces of leaven, can be found in liquor and in many processed foods, which are accordingly proscribed on Pesaḥ.

On the surface, *matzah* represents the cakes that our ancestors baked in haste amid frenetic preparations for departure from the house of bondage. Yet, delving for deeper meanings, the Rabbis identify leaven with the evil inclination, the urge that gives rise to wrongdoing. They point to the philological similarity between the two Hebrew words, *hametz* and *matzah*, and they ponder the implications of this resemblance. It takes mere moments for unleaven to become leaven, and it takes even less time for good intentions to become subverted. The Alexandrian philosopher Philo derives this moral: just as leaven is banned because it is "puffed up," so we must guard against the self-righteousness that puffs us up with false pride.

The lines are drawn—good versus evil, humility versus arrogance, unleaven versus leaven, *matzah* versus *hametz*. A comparison is also made between *matzah*, representing the simple life, and *hametz*, representing the complexities of civilization. Perhaps the temporary "bread embargo" is intended to bring us back to nature and its homespun joys.

Preparing the Seder Table

In honor of this "history feast par excellence," the most momentous meal of the year, it is customary to set the table in festive style, with the finest linen, the finest silverware.

Seder plate—K'arah
The symbols of the Seder are arranged on a sizable dish, preferably a decorative ceremonial platter. (There can be more than one such plate on the table.) The symbols are:

1) *Zeroa* — a roasted bone, usually a shankbone, symbol of the *Pesah* offering. The bone is scorched, to simulate that offering. (Vegetarians may substitute a broiled beet, *Pesahim* 114b.)
2) *Karpas* — a vegetable, usually green.
3) *Haroset* — a mixture of chopped nuts, apples, wine and spices.
4) *Beitzah* — a roasted egg, symbol of the festival offering in the Temple.
5) *Maror* — bitter herbs, either romaine lettuce or horseradish.
6) *Hazeret* (indicated on some Seder plates) — additional *maror* for the *korekh* sandwich.

Matzot. Place three *matzot*, covered, in front of the leader, to the right of the Seder plate. Use plain flour-and-water *matzot* for the Seder. Some people prefer *matzah sh'murah* made with flour which has been guarded since the harvest to prevent fermentation through contact with water. On the day before *Pesah*, some devout Jews bake *matzot* by hand. These are called *matzot mitzvah*.

The Four Cups. Wine punctuates each major section of the Haggadah. Every adult is required to drink these four cups.

Elijah's Cup. A goblet, usually large and ornate, is set aside for Elijah.

Salt water. Karpas is dipped into salt water.

Zeroa, meaning arm, recalls *zeroa netuyah,* the "outstretched arm" and "prodigious acts" with which God redeemed us.

Karpas. Many scholars date this practice back to ancient Rome where banquets would begin with hors d'oeuvres. *Karpas* serves a similar purpose. Green and fresh, it represents the seasonal rebirth of the earth that takes place in spring, the month of Pesah. It also represents the renewal of our hope for redemption.

Hazeret. This term relates to both the Hebrew for "returning/ repentance" and the Aramaic, *hassa,* for "compassion." When we turn to God, He turns to us. When we offer Him an aperture as narrow as a needle's eye, He opens a door as wide as a palace portal. But while it is normally necessary for us to take the initiative, in Mitzrayim God compassionately bypassed this requirement. He Himself initiated and accelerated our redemption.

The Four Cups. Red wine is preferred. But it is sobering to recall that during the Dark Ages, when the ritual murder accusation was rife, some Seder celebrants would deliberately opt for white wine to disassociate Pesah proceedings totally from that grotesque indictment.

Salt water. What could be more humdrum than salt? But at the Seder even salt is seasoned with ramifications historic and folkloric. Salt recalls slavery's tears and Temple pageantry (since salt accompanied the offerings). A preservative, salt is a symbol of permanence, the immutability of the covenant. And it reminds us that Sodom and Gomorrah were turned into saltlands (according to rabbinic tradition, this happened on Pesah) because their inhabitants behaved so viciously towards strangers. Notions worth their salt.

Reclining. We sit back at ease, in cushioned comfort, like Solomon in his royal residence (Song of Songs 1:12), or like patricians in ancient Greece and Rome, dining in state, recumbent on couches. It has been suggested that leaning, *m'subin*, means more than *reclin*ing; that it implies *in*clining. We lean towards each other as we enter, wakefully and willingly, into "the order of history."

HISTORICAL NOTE: In Plato's Athens, philosophers and men of letters would convene in each other's homes for freewheeling debate, interspersing epicurean collation with pithy conversation. The Greeks had a word for such a gathering: symposium. And since the Rabbis of old were adept at adopting and transfiguring the customs of secular society, some scholars see the symposium as the model for our Seder. There is, of course, a world of difference. The Seder breathes a degree of democracy unheard of in the Graeco-Roman world. The Seder is an equal-opportunity celebration, both a reenactment of history and a reaffirmation of faith, both a national commemoration and a family affair involving every man, woman and child in the community. All are invited, all are welcome, all are equal.

Reclining. It is customary to recline during the Seder, in an armchair or against pillows.

Kittel. Some leaders don a white robe called a *kittel*. White is the color of joy, of freedom and festivity. In the kabbalistic color spectrum, white represents mercy and lovingkindness, the divine attributes to which we attribute our deliverance from Mitzrayim. The *kittel* is a reminder of the vestments of the Temple priests and of the raiment worn by the ancient Israelites on festivals. "The people wear white, eat and drink and rejoice, for they know that the Holy One, praised be He, performs miracles for them."

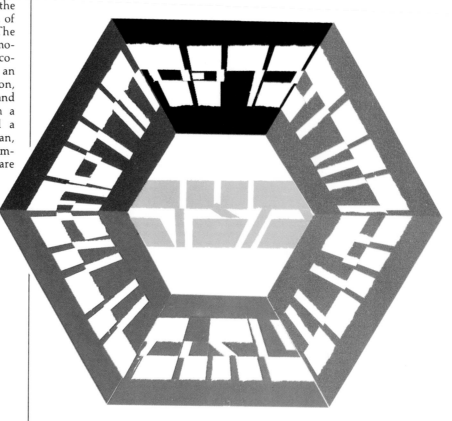

Before sunset, light the candles and recite:

בָּרוּךְ אַתָּה יהוה אֱלֹהֵינוּ מֶלֶךְ הָעוֹלָם אֲשֶׁר קִדְּשָׁנוּ
בְּמִצְוֹתָיו וְצִוָּנוּ לְהַדְלִיק נֵר שֶׁל (שַׁבָּת וְשֶׁל) יוֹם טוֹב.

Those who recite the second blessing (she-heheyanu) at this point need not repeat it during Kiddush.

בָּרוּךְ אַתָּה יהוה אֱלֹהֵינוּ מֶלֶךְ הָעוֹלָם שֶׁהֶחֱיָנוּ
וְקִיְּמָנוּ וְהִגִּיעָנוּ לַזְּמַן הַזֶּה.

Candle Lighting

Let there be light. When we kindle these candles, we recall, albeit briefly, the primordial light that once illuminated the world from end to end. When the first man and the first woman rebelled in Eden, they bedimmed the light and it disappeared from human sight. Not until the Messiah comes will that lucent light shine forth again. Meanwhile, Shabbat and yom tov bring us glimmerings of messianic brightness.

Before sunset, light the candles and recite:

Praised are You, Adonai our God, King of the universe who has sanctified our lives through His commandments, commanding us to kindle the (Shabbat and) festival lights.

Those who recite the second blessing (she-heḥeyanu) at this point need not repeat it during Kiddush.

Praised are You, Adonai our God, King of the universe, for giving us life, for sustaining us and for enabling us to celebrate this festival.

Every edition of the Haggadah looks different. Every reading sounds different, suggesting new nuances, new insights. Yet the Seder, the ordering of the evening, has changed little since it was orchestrated by the masters of the Mishnah so many centuries ago. It is hardly happenstance that the Seder has become such a rare fusion of fixity and flux, of structure and spontaneity. For while it is meritorious to elaborate upon the Exodus, it is mandatory to observe the basics. To ensure that these basics were preserved, at a time when not every Jew possessed a Haggadah, the Rabbis devised an aide-mémoire, a rhymed mnemonic, which is often chanted as a prelude to the Seder.

KADESH

URHATZ

KARPAS

YAHATZ

MAGGID

ROHTZAH

MOTZI

MATZAH

MAROR

KOREKH

SHULHAN OREKH

TZAFUN

BAREKH

HALLEL

NIRTZAH

הִנְנִי מוּכָן/מוּכָנָה וּמְזֻמָּן/וּמְזֻמֶּנֶת לְקַיֵּם מִצְוַת כּוֹס רִאשׁוֹן שֶׁהוּא כְּנֶגֶד בְּשׂוֹרַת הַיְשׁוּעָה, שֶׁאָמַר הַקָּדוֹשׁ בָּרוּךְ הוּא לְיִשְׂרָאֵל: וְהוֹצֵאתִי אֶתְכֶם מִתַּחַת סִבְלֹת מִצְרָיִם.

Lift the cup of wine and recite Kiddush, adding the words in parentheses on Shabbat.

(וַיַּרְא אֱלֹהִים אֶת כָּל אֲשֶׁר עָשָׂה וְהִנֵּה טוֹב מְאֹד, וַיְהִי עֶרֶב וַיְהִי בֹקֶר יוֹם הַשִּׁשִּׁי. וַיְכֻלּוּ הַשָּׁמַיִם וְהָאָרֶץ וְכָל צְבָאָם. וַיְכַל אֱלֹהִים בַּיּוֹם הַשְּׁבִיעִי מְלַאכְתּוֹ אֲשֶׁר עָשָׂה, וַיִּשְׁבֹּת בַּיּוֹם הַשְּׁבִיעִי מִכָּל מְלַאכְתּוֹ אֲשֶׁר עָשָׂה. וַיְבָרֶךְ אֱלֹהִים אֶת יוֹם הַשְּׁבִיעִי וַיְקַדֵּשׁ אֹתוֹ, כִּי בוֹ שָׁבַת מִכָּל מְלַאכְתּוֹ אֲשֶׁר בָּרָא אֱלֹהִים לַעֲשׂוֹת.)

סָבְרִי מָרָנָן:

בָּרוּךְ אַתָּה יהוה אֱלֹהֵינוּ מֶלֶךְ הָעוֹלָם בּוֹרֵא פְּרִי הַגָּפֶן.

בָּרוּךְ אַתָּה יהוה אֱלֹהֵינוּ מֶלֶךְ הָעוֹלָם אֲשֶׁר בָּחַר בָּנוּ מִכָּל עָם וְרוֹמְמָנוּ מִכָּל לָשׁוֹן וְקִדְּשָׁנוּ בְּמִצְוֹתָיו. וַתִּתֶּן לָנוּ יהוה אֱלֹהֵינוּ בְּאַהֲבָה (שַׁבָּתוֹת לִמְנוּחָה וּ)מוֹעֲדִים לְשִׂמְחָה, חַגִּים וּזְמַנִּים לְשָׂשׂוֹן, אֶת יוֹם (הַשַּׁבָּת הַזֶּה וְאֶת יוֹם) חַג הַמַּצּוֹת הַזֶּה, זְמַן חֵרוּתֵנוּ, (בְּאַהֲבָה) מִקְרָא קֹדֶשׁ, זֵכֶר לִיצִיאַת מִצְרָיִם. כִּי בָנוּ בָחַרְתָּ, וְאוֹתָנוּ קִדַּשְׁתָּ, מִכָּל הָעַמִּים (וְשַׁבָּת) וּמוֹעֲדֵי קָדְשֶׁךָ (בְּאַהֲבָה וּבְרָצוֹן) בְּשִׂמְחָה וּבְשָׂשׂוֹן הִנְחַלְתָּנוּ. בָּרוּךְ אַתָּה יהוה מְקַדֵּשׁ (הַשַּׁבָּת וְ)יִשְׂרָאֵל וְהַזְּמַנִּים.

WHY: *Kiddush* is recited on the eve of every Shabbat and every festival, customarily over a brimming cup of wine, a symbol of joy, as it is written, "wine gladdens the heart of man" (Psalms 104:15). Tonight, *Kiddush* is recited over the first of the Four Cups.

WHY is wine used as a symbol of sanctification when it so readily brings to mind revelry and intoxication? How can it be a symbol of liberation when so many have become enslaved to it? The point is that, in Jewish tradition, no object is intrinsically good or intrinsically bad. Its nature is determined by the way we use — or misuse — it.

Sanctifying the seventh day. The seventh day is the armistice in man's cruel struggle for existence, a truce in all conflicts, personal and social . . . a day on which handling money is considered a desecration, on which man avows his independence of that which is the world's chief idol. The seventh day is the exodus from tension, the installation of man as a sovereign in the world of time.

Shabbat and Shapatu. It is instructive to compare Shapatu, celebrated every seventh day of a moon-month by the ancient Babylonians, with this uniquely Jewish institution, the incomparable Shabbat. Shapatu was dedicated to Saturn (hence Saturn's day or Saturday). In the old astrological tradition, Saturn was the lord of time, the lord of death, the lord whose fury and malevolence had to be propitiated by mourning and self-castigation. Sinister and cheerless were the shadows cast by Saturn, in startling contradistinction to the light and joy radiating from Shabbat. On this hallowed day, Saturn is dethroned, mourning is transcended, time is suspended. Goodness and gladness prevail. Life and love and freedom reign supreme.

You have favored us with Shabbat. An everlasting reminder of the Exodus, Shabbat liberates us from the trammels of time and toil. Week after week, Shabbat proclaims that every individual, including the strangers in our midst and the very beasts of the field, enjoy equal rights before God. Shabbat, one of God's greatest gifts to Israel, is one of Israel's greatest gifts to humanity. Shabbat spans the ages, from the beginning of time to the End of Days. In its observance we become partners in creation, and in its transcendent tranquillity we glimpse the world to come.

Commemorating the Exodus. The recitation of *Kiddush*, which always includes the phrase *yetziyat Mitzrayim*, has far-reaching reverberations at the Seder, building bridges — triumphs of spiritual engineering — that span the Exodus and all the festivals of the Jewish year. Both the giving of the Torah on Shavuot and the wandering in the desert on Sukkot are related to an event so epochal that all events in Jewish history are connected to it. This is understandable, for the event is nothing less than the birth of the Jewish people, chosen by God and redeemed by Him from the crucible of Egyptian slavery.

You have chosen us. The doctrine of Israel as the Chosen People is not true because it is an article of faith; it is an article of faith because it is true. The singular character of the Jewish group is neither an expression of group conceit nor a figment of the historical imagination, nor a mere theological doctrine. It is an empirical fact, the logical consequence of thirty-five hundred years of a special history which mirrors an experience unparalleled in any other society.

Kadesh

Reflection:

I am ready to fulfill the commandment of drinking the first of the Four Cups. This recalls God's promise of redemption to the people Israel, as it says, "I will free you from the burden of the Egyptians" (Exodus 6:6).

Lift the cup of wine and recite Kiddush, adding the words in parentheses on Shabbat.

(And God saw all that He had made, and found it very good. And there was evening and there was morning, the sixth day. The heavens and the earth, and all they contain, were completed. On the seventh day God finished the work which He had been doing. He rested on the seventh day from all the work which He had done. Then God blessed the seventh day and sanctified it, because on it He rested from all His work of creation.)

Praised are You, Adonai our God, King of the universe who creates the fruit of the vine.

Praised are You, Adonai our God, King of the universe who has chosen us and distinguished us by sanctifying us through His commandments. You have lovingly favored us with (Shabbat for rest and) festivals for joy, seasons and holidays for happiness, among them (this Shabbat and) this day of Pesaḥ, the season of our liberation, a day of sacred assembly commemorating the Exodus from Mitzrayim. You have chosen us, sanctifying us among all peoples by granting us (Shabbat and) Your sacred festivals (lovingly and gladly) in joy and happiness. Praised are You, Adonai who sanctifies (Shabbat and) the people Israel and the festival seasons.

On Saturday night (motza-ei Shabbat), add:

בָּרוּךְ אַתָּה יהוה אֱלֹהֵינוּ מֶלֶךְ הָעוֹלָם בּוֹרֵא מְאוֹרֵי הָאֵשׁ.

בָּרוּךְ אַתָּה יהוה אֱלֹהֵינוּ מֶלֶךְ הָעוֹלָם הַמַּבְדִּיל בֵּין קֹדֶשׁ לְחוֹל, בֵּין אוֹר לְחֹשֶׁךְ, בֵּין יִשְׂרָאֵל לָעַמִּים, בֵּין יוֹם הַשְּׁבִיעִי לְשֵׁשֶׁת יְמֵי הַמַּעֲשֶׂה, בֵּין קְדֻשַּׁת שַׁבָּת לִקְדֻשַּׁת יוֹם טוֹב הִבְדַּלְתָּ, וְאֶת יוֹם הַשְּׁבִיעִי מִשֵּׁשֶׁת יְמֵי הַמַּעֲשֶׂה קִדַּשְׁתָּ, הִבְדַּלְתָּ וְקִדַּשְׁתָּ אֶת עַמְּךָ יִשְׂרָאֵל בִּקְדֻשָּׁתֶךָ. בָּרוּךְ אַתָּה יהוה הַמַּבְדִּיל בֵּין קֹדֶשׁ לְקֹדֶשׁ.

בָּרוּךְ אַתָּה יהוה אֱלֹהֵינוּ מֶלֶךְ הָעוֹלָם שֶׁהֶחֱיָנוּ וְקִיְּמָנוּ וְהִגִּיעָנוּ לַזְּמַן הַזֶּה.

Drink the wine while reclining.

Wash your hands without reciting the customary blessing.

Dip a vegetable in salt water and recite:

בָּרוּךְ אַתָּה יהוה אֱלֹהֵינוּ מֶלֶךְ הָעוֹלָם בּוֹרֵא פְּרִי הָאֲדָמָה.

Take the middle matzah and break it in two. Wrap the larger piece in a napkin and set it aside as the afikomen, to be eaten at the conclusion of the meal. Replace the smaller piece between the other two matzot. It is customary to hide the afikomen, and in some families the children hold it for ransom.

WHY: *Havdalah* customarily comprises blessings over wine, over spices and over fire. Here only the latter is recited, for the blessing over wine is included in the *Kiddush*, and the blessing over spices is applicable only when Shabbat is followed by an ordinary workday. This *Havdalah* marks the transition from Shabbat to yom tov.

Yaknehaz is a handy mnemonic that helps to register the sequence of the *Kiddush* blessings when yom tov begins on Saturday night (*motza-ei Shabbat*): *yayin* (wine), *kiddush* (sanctification), *ner* (light), *havdalah* (end of Shabbat) and finally *z'man* (*sheheheyanu*). Because it sounds like the German phrase *jag den Has*, "hunt the hare," some medieval artists enlivened their Haggadot with a hare-hunting scene, a double anomaly since hunting animals is unJewish and the hare is "unclean" to boot. This linguistic fabrication was absorbed into the vernacular, and a fictional village called Yaknehaz became the setting for some of Sholom Aleichem's stories.

Fire. Adam came into being just before dusk on the sixth day of creation. When he saw the sun vanish and blackness blanket the earth, he was terrified. Then God showed him how to dispel darkness and fear. By rubbing together two flintstones, Night and Death's Shadow, Adam created fire.

Differentiating. The Torah teaches us to make distinctions. We are bidden by revelation to distinguish between God and idols, between true and false prophets, between pure and impure, between good and evil, between sacred and profane; in sum, between that which conforms to God and that which does not conform to Him. Our destiny — our very survival — depends on whether we make the right distinctions.

You hallowed Your people Israel. We are God's stake in human history. We are the dawn and the dusk, the challenge and the test. How strange to be a Jew and to go astray on God's perilous errands. We have been offered as a pattern of worship and as a prey for scorn, but there is more still in our destiny. We carry the gold of God in our souls to forge the gate of the kingdom.

Peoplehood, personhood. On this night of bonding, of unity and community, we gather together to celebrate our birth as a nation, to review our historic heritage, to ratify our collective covenant. But, at the same time, each of us must make a personal statement of accountability and commitment. For while Judaism fosters a strong sense of peoplehood, of *klal Yisrael*, it also insists on individual responsibility, on individual worth.

Adonai differentiates. When a person strikes many coins from one mold, they all resemble one another. The supreme King of kings fashions every man in the stamp of the first man, yet not one resembles his fellow. Therefore every human being is obliged to say, "The world was created for my sake."

HOW: Using a pitcher or a cup, pour water over each hand. Why are "washing instructions" pertinent? Because this is an act of ritual cleansing. All the participants may wash their hands, or the leader may do so on their behalf before distributing *karpas*.

HOW: A vegetable, preferably a green vegetable, like parsley, is dipped in salt water. (This is the first dipping.) Some people recline while eating *karpas*.

WHY: Why is the *afikomen* wrapped up? One explanation links this to the manner in which the Israelites left Mitzrayim, with their kneading utensils wrapped in their garments (Exodus 12:34).

On Saturday night (motza-ei Shabbat), add:

Praised are You, Adonai our God, King of the universe who creates the lights of fire.

Praised are You, Adonai our God, King of the universe who differentiates between sacred and profane, between light and darkness, between Israel and other nations, between the seventh day and the six days of creating. You made a distinction between the sanctity of Shabbat and the sanctity of the festivals, and You sanctified Shabbat more than the other days of the week, distinguishing and hallowing Your people Israel through Your holiness. Praised are You, Adonai who differentiates between the sanctity of Shabbat and the sanctity of yom tov.

Praised are You, Adonai our God, King of the universe, for giving us life, for sustaining us and for enabling us to celebrate this festival.

Drink the wine while reclining.

Urhatz

Wash your hands without reciting the customary blessing.

Karpas

Dip a vegetable in salt water and recite:

Praised are You, Adonai our God, King of the universe who creates the fruit of the earth.

Yahatz

Take the middle matzah and break it in two. Wrap the larger piece in a napkin and set it aside as the afikomen, to be eaten at the conclusion of the meal. Replace the smaller piece between the other two matzot. It is customary to hide the afikomen, and in some families the children hold it for ransom.

WHY: Why are three *matzot* used? Two loaves are traditional for Shabbat and festivals, visual reminders of the double portion of "heavenly bread" that the Israelites would gather every sixth day during those decades of desert wayfaring, since no manna appeared on Shabbat. A third *matzah* is added on Pesaḥ to represent the bread of affliction (*leḥem oni*), which is divided at this point. Most authorities believe that the *matzah* we break for *yaḥatz* cannot be used for the *motzi* blessing before the meal; hence the additional *matzah*.

The stacked *matzot* can be taken to represent both the divisions (Kohanim, Levites, Israelites) and the unity of the Jewish people. The three *matzot* are also reminiscent of the "three measures of fine meal" from which, at Abraham's request, Sarah baked instant cakes for their three angelic visitors (Genesis 18:6).

WHY: Why do we break the middle *matzah*? A symbol of the skimpy fare upon which we subsisted as slaves, *matzah* is broken in half to dramatize its pitiful inadequacy. "Breaking bread" also signifies hospitality, and we are about to invite the needy and the hungry to eat with us and to share with us.

Unleavened bread is the leveler that raises us all to the same lofty level. Outside, the battle rages between the haves and the have-nots, between those who have more and those who have less. Too often the struggle for daily bread is attended by feverish competition, tension and trauma. But at this most egalitarian of banquets, bread of the most unpretentious kind is the uncommon denominator that makes all Israel *ḥaverim* (kin).

Uncover the matzot.

הָא לַחְמָא עַנְיָא
דִּי אֲכָלוּ אַבְהָתָנָא בְּאַרְעָא דְמִצְרָיִם.
כָּל דִּכְפִין יֵיתֵי וְיֵכֻל,
כָּל דִּצְרִיךְ יֵיתֵי וְיִפְסַח.
הָשַׁתָּא הָכָא, לַשָּׁנָה הַבָּאָה בְּאַרְעָא דְיִשְׂרָאֵל.
הָשַׁתָּא עַבְדֵי, לַשָּׁנָה הַבָּאָה בְּנֵי חוֹרִין.

In the hope that next year all Jews, and indeed all humanity, will be free, we utter a plea for those around the world who are persecuted and unfree.

יְהִי רָצוֹן מִלְפָנֶיךָ יהוה אֱלֹהֵינוּ וֵאלֹהֵי אֲבוֹתֵינוּ שֶׁכְּמוֹ
שֶׁלָּקַחְתָּ גוֹי מִקֶּרֶב גוֹי וְהֶעֱבַרְתָּ אֶת עַמְּךָ יִשְׂרָאֵל בְּתוֹךְ הַיָּם,
כֵּן תְּרַחֵם עַל אַחֵינוּ כָּל בֵּית יִשְׂרָאֵל הַנְּתוּנִים בְּצָרָה וּבְשִׁבְיָה,
הָעוֹמְדִים בֵּין בַּיָּם וּבֵין בַּיַּבָּשָׁה. תַּצִילֵם וְתוֹצִיאֵם מִצָּרָה
לִרְוָחָה וּמֵאֲפֵלָה לְאוֹרָה וּמִשִׁעְבּוּד לִגְאֻלָּה, בִּמְהֵרָה בְיָמֵינוּ
וְנֹאמַר אָמֵן.

WHY: Few things reveal more about the character of the redactors of the Haggadah than the fact that this overture to the poor and to the stranger is couched in Aramaic, the language spoken by Jews in talmudic times. It was regarded as imperative that the invitation should be understood by everyone. For the very same reason, some recite this paragraph in English as well.

The theme of hospitality is threaded through the Seder, through Pesaḥ, through all our festivals. We open our homes to those who are homeless, and we open our door to Elijah, symbol of the weary wayfarer. Moreover, these symbolic gestures are prefaced by practical measures.

Before Pesaḥ we collect and distribute *maot ḥittin* (literally "money for grain"), so that every Jew should be free to celebrate the festival of freedom. *Halakhah* prescribes that *matzah* and wine for the Four Cups must be provided for even the poorest among us, those who subsist solely on charity. To allow any Jew to suffer deprivation on this day would be a mockery of Pesaḥ, for it would mean that we had forgotten that we were all once slaves in Mitzrayim.

This is the bread of affliction. Why do we start this joyous celebration with a pointed reference to the bread of affliction? Perhaps we do so to underscore that many of our fellow Jews are still afflicted, that there is still hunger in the world, and that we are still in exile (*galut*). This pivotal passage culminates in a confident assertion of our belief that the redemption will come and will come soon.

Leḥem oni, "the bread over which much is answered," lies before us, flat yet dimensional, poor by gastronomic standards yet rich in storied associations. Could there be a more suitable symbol for this night of contrasts, show-and-tell, questioning and quest?

Let them enter and eat. . . . let them celebrate Pesaḥ. The first phrase deals with material needs, the second with spiritual needs. One school of thought maintains that physical freedom must precede metaphysical freedom. First we left Mitzrayim, then we received the Torah at Sinai. The opposing school of thought argues that only an ardent yearning for emancipation can pave the way for the actual act of emancipation.

Next year in the land of Israel. Even as we look back at the Exodus, we look forward to redemption in the future. The Seder begins and ends with the same vision — next year in Jerusalem, or, as Jews in Israel proclaim, "Next year in Jerusalem rebuilt."

Jerusalem. Surely no city in the world has inspired greater passion. For three thousand years, with a loyalty beyond belief and almost beyond reason, we have dreamed of it and died for it, loved it, longed for it, lamented over it, celebrated it in our liturgy and our literature and our everyday lives, setting it always above our chiefest joy. While we prayed daily for reunion with our divinely consecrated capital, the earthly Jerusalem, we also envisioned an other-worldly Jerusalem on high. Yet the reality, the tangible temporal city cascading over the Judean hills, was never overshadowed by the mythic metropolis in the clouds. "I shall enter the heavenly Jerusalem," declared the Holy One, praised be He, "only after My children enter Jerusalem on earth" (Zohar 1:1b).

Maggid

Uncover the matzot.

This is the bread of affliction
which our ancestors ate in the land of Mitzrayim.
All who are hungry, let them enter and eat.
All who are in need, let them come celebrate Pesaḥ.
Now we are here. Next year in the land of Israel.
Now we are enslaved. Next year we will be free.

In the hope that next year all Jews, and indeed all humanity, will be free, we utter a plea for those around the world who are persecuted and unfree.

Adonai, our God and God of our ancestors, just as You took the Israelites from among the Egyptians and led them through the sea, so may You have mercy on our brothers and sisters, the House of Israel, those who are distressed and those who are oppressed, wherever they may be. Save them. Lead them from narrow straits to abundant favor, from darkness to light, from enslavement to redemption, speedily, in our days, and let us say: Amen.

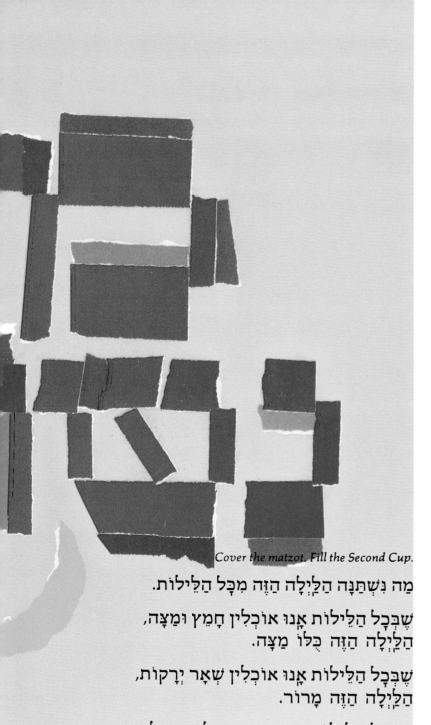

Cover the matzot. Fill the Second Cup.

מַה נִּשְׁתַּנָּה הַלַּיְלָה הַזֶּה מִכָּל הַלֵּילוֹת.

שֶׁבְּכָל הַלֵּילוֹת אָנוּ אוֹכְלִין חָמֵץ וּמַצָּה,
הַלַּיְלָה הַזֶּה כֻּלּוֹ מַצָּה.

שֶׁבְּכָל הַלֵּילוֹת אָנוּ אוֹכְלִין שְׁאָר יְרָקוֹת,
הַלַּיְלָה הַזֶּה מָרוֹר.

שֶׁבְּכָל הַלֵּילוֹת אֵין אָנוּ מַטְבִּילִין אֲפִילוּ פַּעַם אֶחָת,
הַלַּיְלָה הַזֶּה שְׁתֵּי פְעָמִים.

שֶׁבְּכָל הַלֵּילוֹת אָנוּ אוֹכְלִין בֵּין יוֹשְׁבִין וּבֵין מְסֻבִּין,
הַלַּיְלָה הַזֶּה כֻּלָּנוּ מְסֻבִּין.

HOW: It is the custom for the youngest child to ask the Four Questions. Actually, the Talmud states that *anyone* can ask them, even a scholar at the table of scholars, or, since the questions are somewhat rhetorical, a lone person celebrating a Seder. The Four Questions were originally meant to be sample questions, but later they became integrated into the ritual. The Talmud relates that Abbaye was once present at a Seder with his teacher Rabbah. When the dish with Pesaḥ foods was removed, Abbaye exclaimed: "We have not yet eaten. Why have they taken away the dish?" Rabbah replied: "You have exempted us from reciting *Mah nishtanah*" (*Pesaḥim* 115b). From this incident we deduce that any relevant questions can serve as starting points.

HISTORICAL NOTE: In Temple times there were only three questions; they referred to (1) *matzah*, (2) dipping twice, and (3) the roasting of the *Pesaḥ* offering. When dipping food, once standard practice at meals, was no longer fashionable, the second question was modified. After the destruction of the Temple, a question about *maror* was substituted for the question dealing with sacrifices. The question about reclining was added at a later date.

Factors psychological as well as logical determine the protocol of the Seder. The meal used to come before the Four Questions so that these could reasonably relate to foods which had already been eaten. But it seemed to the sages that the attention of the participants waned after the wining and dining, and so the narration was advanced and the repast was delayed.

The Four Questions. Why are these questions asked and never directly answered in the Haggadah? To this question there are more than four answers.

1. Questioning is a sign of freedom, proof that we are free to investigate, to analyze, to satisfy our intellectual curiosity.

2. The simplest question can have many answers, sometimes complex and contradictory ones, even as life itself is fraught with complexity and contradictions. To see everything as good or bad, *matzah* or *maror*, is to be enslaved to simplicity.

3. The Haggadah challenges us to ask ourselves whether we are asking the right questions.

4. To accept the fact that not every question has an answer, that not every problem can be neatly resolved, is another stage of liberation. In the same way that questioning is a sign of freedom, acknowledging that some things are beyond our understanding is a sign of faith. Says Rabbi Wolfe of Zhitomir: "For the believer, there is no question; for the non-believer, there is no answer."

5. When we find the answers for ourselves, we find ourselves experiencing and understanding the true meaning of the Exodus.

The forty-nine questions. "To attain truth," says Rabbi Barukh of Medzebezh, "man must pass forty-nine gates, each opening to a new question. Finally he arrives at the last gate, the last question, beyond which he could not live without faith."

Cover the matzot. Fill the Second Cup.

How different this night is from all other nights!

On all other nights we eat either *ḥametz* or *matzah*.
  Why, on this night, do we eat only *matzah*?

On all other nights we eat all kinds of vegetables.
  Why, on this night, must we eat bitter herbs?

On all other nights we do not usually dip vegetables even once.
  Why, on this night, do we dip twice?

On all other nights we eat either sitting upright or reclining.
  Why, on this night, do we eat reclining?

עֲבָדִים הָיִינוּ

Uncover the matzot.

עֲבָדִים הָיִינוּ לְפַרְעֹה בְּמִצְרָיִם. וַיּוֹצִיאֵנוּ יְהוָה אֱלֹהֵינוּ מִשָּׁם בְּיָד חֲזָקָה וּבִזְרוֹעַ נְטוּיָה. וְאִלּוּ לֹא הוֹצִיא הַקָּדוֹשׁ בָּרוּךְ הוּא אֶת אֲבוֹתֵינוּ מִמִּצְרַיִם, הֲרֵי אָנוּ וּבָנֵינוּ וּבְנֵי בָנֵינוּ מְשֻׁעְבָּדִים הָיִינוּ לְפַרְעֹה בְּמִצְרָיִם. וַאֲפִלּוּ כֻּלָּנוּ חֲכָמִים, כֻּלָּנוּ נְבוֹנִים, כֻּלָּנוּ זְקֵנִים, כֻּלָּנוּ יוֹדְעִים אֶת הַתּוֹרָה, מִצְוָה עָלֵינוּ לְסַפֵּר בִּיצִיאַת מִצְרָיִם. וְכָל הַמַּרְבֶּה לְסַפֵּר בִּיצִיאַת מִצְרַיִם הֲרֵי זֶה מְשֻׁבָּח.

מַעֲשֶׂה בְּרַבִּי אֱלִיעֶזֶר וְרַבִּי יְהוֹשֻׁעַ וְרַבִּי אֶלְעָזָר בֶּן עֲזַרְיָה וְרַבִּי עֲקִיבָא וְרַבִּי טַרְפוֹן, שֶׁהָיוּ מְסֻבִּין בִּבְנֵי בְרַק, וְהָיוּ מְסַפְּרִים בִּיצִיאַת מִצְרַיִם כָּל אוֹתוֹ הַלַּיְלָה, עַד שֶׁבָּאוּ תַלְמִידֵיהֶם וְאָמְרוּ לָהֶם: רַבּוֹתֵינוּ, הִגִּיעַ זְמַן קְרִיאַת שְׁמַע שֶׁל שַׁחֲרִית.

אָמַר רַבִּי אֶלְעָזָר בֶּן עֲזַרְיָה: הֲרֵי אֲנִי כְּבֶן שִׁבְעִים שָׁנָה. וְלֹא זָכִיתִי שֶׁתֵּאָמֵר יְצִיאַת מִצְרַיִם בַּלֵּילוֹת, עַד שֶׁדְּרָשָׁהּ בֶּן זוֹמָא, שֶׁנֶּאֱמַר: לְמַעַן תִּזְכֹּר אֶת יוֹם צֵאתְךָ מֵאֶרֶץ מִצְרַיִם כֹּל יְמֵי חַיֶּיךָ. יְמֵי חַיֶּיךָ — הַיָּמִים. כֹּל יְמֵי חַיֶּיךָ — הַלֵּילוֹת. וַחֲכָמִים אוֹמְרִים: יְמֵי חַיֶּיךָ — הָעוֹלָם הַזֶּה. כֹּל יְמֵי חַיֶּיךָ — לְהָבִיא לִימוֹת הַמָּשִׁיחַ.

We were slaves. Our ancestors served idols (see page 43). The momentous multiple meanings of the Seder are synthesized in the relationship between these two apparently unrelated statements, flashbacks, recalling our inglorious past. For to say that we celebrate our deliverance from slavery is both an oversimplification and an understatement. On the one hand, we celebrate freedom on a physical, political and national level, freedom springing from a climactic happening in the history of our people—and of the world. On the other hand, we also celebrate the spiritual, personal and religious aspects that constitute the overriding reason for the Exodus: God's choice of Israel as His witnesses. As a result of the Exodus, we became a nation dedicated to God, devoted to His service and His Torah.

WHY: The Four Questions really amount to one question—why do we celebrate Pesaḥ? In addressing this issue, the Haggadah conforms to the talmudic principle, "Begin with degradation and end with glory" (*Pesaḥim* 116a). The meaning of degradation is debated in the Talmud by Rav and Samuel. Since Samuel equates degradation with slavery, he thinks we should start by reciting "We were slaves" (*Avadim hayinu*). Since Rav equates degradation with idolatry, he advocates starting with "In the beginning our ancestors served idols" (*Mitehilah*). We read both passages at the Seder because both passages are equally relevant. From slavery to idolatry is a movement back in time from the Exodus to Abraham, who set our saga in motion, for he set the scene for ultimate redemption when he rejected his father's gods.

Adonai brought us forth. God set an example by freeing a people from slavery, demonstrating that slavery is not an irreversible condition, that freedom is not an unattainable ideal. Since the Exodus, writes the poet Heine, Freedom has always spoken with a Hebrew accent.

A tale is told. Many inferences can be drawn from this seemingly straightforward account of how these five celebrated sages celebrated the Seder in B'nei B'rak during the beginning of the second century of the common era. It underlines the importance of the *mitzvah* of telling the Exodus story, and how much there is to tell. For so absorbing was the discussion that it lasted until daybreak. Incidentally, these same scholars, Rabbi Akiva and Rabbi Tarfon in particular, were instrumental in incorporating into the Seder service such passages as *Dayyenu* and the text of the blessing on redemption.

One hypothesis submits that the five elders were planning the revolt of Bar Kokhba against the Romans (132–135 C.E.) in which Rabbi Akiva played a prominent role. Perhaps, then, the students' reminder about the morning *Sh'ma* was a password, signaling the approach of Roman soldiers.

It has also been suggested that this was "a summit meeting," a crisis session to examine ways and means of dealing with a relatively unfamiliar predicament: exile. How should the Jewish people respond? Should they resist openly? Or in secret? Should they cooperate? And, if so, to what degree? And how could they remain Jewish in a hostile non-Jewish environment? Unhappily, Rabbi Eliezer and his colleagues were neither the first nor the last to grapple with these dilemmas.

We were slaves

Uncover the matzot.

We were slaves to Pharaoh in Mitzrayim but Adonai our God brought us forth with a mighty hand and with an outstretched arm. And if the Holy One, praised be He, had not taken our ancestors out of Mitzrayim, then we, and our children, and our children's children, would still be enslaved to Pharaoh in Mitzrayim. Now even if all of us were scholars, even if all of us were sages, even if all of us were elders, even if all of us were learned in the Torah, it would still be our duty to tell the story of the Exodus from Mitzrayim. Moreover, whoever elaborates upon the story of the Exodus deserves praise.

A tale is told about Rabbi Eliezer, Rabbi Joshua, Rabbi Elazar ben Azariah, Rabbi Akiva and Rabbi Tarfon. They were gathered in B'nei B'rak, discussing the Exodus from Mitzrayim all through the night, until their students came to them and said, "Masters, the time has come to recite the morning *Sh'ma.*"

Rabbi Elazar ben Azariah said, "Behold, I am as old as the years of man, yet I was not convinced that the Exodus should be referred to every night until ben Zoma explained it to me through this verse, 'In order that you may remember the day of your departure from Mitzrayim all the days of your life' (Deuteronomy 16:3). 'The days of your life' indicates only during the day. 'All the days of your life' includes the night as well." The sages explain, "'The days of your life' means in this world. 'All the days of your life' includes the days of the Messiah."

בָּרוּךְ הַמָּקוֹם.

בָּרוּךְ הוּא.

בָּרוּךְ שֶׁנָּתַן תּוֹרָה לְעַמּוֹ יִשְׂרָאֵל.

בָּרוּךְ הוּא.

כְּנֶגֶד אַרְבָּעָה בָנִים דִּבְּרָה תוֹרָה.

אֶחָד חָכָם

וְאֶחָד רָשָׁע

וְאֶחָד תָּם

וְאֶחָד שֶׁאֵינוֹ יוֹדֵעַ לִשְׁאוֹל.

חָכָם מַה הוּא אוֹמֵר? מָה הָעֵדֹת וְהַחֻקִּים וְהַמִּשְׁפָּטִים אֲשֶׁר צִוָּה יְהוָה אֱלֹהֵינוּ אֹתָנוּ? וְאַף אַתָּה אֱמָר לוֹ כְּהִלְכוֹת הַפֶּסַח עַד: אֵין מַפְטִירִין בָּאֹכֶל אַחַר הָאֲפִיקוֹמָן.

רָשָׁע מַה הוּא אוֹמֵר? מָה הָעֲבֹדָה הַזֹּאת לָכֶם? לָכֶם וְלֹא לוֹ. וּלְפִי שֶׁהוֹצִיא אֶת עַצְמוֹ מִן הַכְּלָל כָּפַר בְּעִקָּר. וְאַף אַתָּה הַקְהֵה אֶת שִׁנָּיו וֶאֱמָר לוֹ: בַּעֲבוּר זֶה עָשָׂה יְהוָה לִי בְּצֵאתִי מִמִּצְרָיִם. לִי וְלֹא לוֹ. אִלּוּ הָיָה שָׁם, לֹא הָיָה נִגְאָל.

תָּם מַה הוּא אוֹמֵר? מַה זֹּאת? וְאָמַרְתָּ אֵלָיו: בְּחֹזֶק יָד הוֹצִיאָנוּ יְהוָה מִמִּצְרָיִם מִבֵּית עֲבָדִים.

וְשֶׁאֵינוֹ יוֹדֵעַ לִשְׁאוֹל, אַתְּ פְּתַח לוֹ, שֶׁנֶּאֱמַר: וְהִגַּדְתָּ לְבִנְךָ בַּיּוֹם הַהוּא לֵאמֹר, בַּעֲבוּר זֶה עָשָׂה יְהוָה לִי בְּצֵאתִי מִמִּצְרָיִם.

He who is everywhere. This name of God, *haMakom*, meaning The Place, reflects the Jewish perception of the universality as well as the ubiquity of the God of Israel. He contains, yet cannot be contained. He surrounds, yet cannot be surrounded. His place is everywhere (even in the lowliest thornbush), yet no one knows where He is, or where He is not. "He is the place of the world, yet the world alone is not His place."

Where I wander—You.
Where I ponder—You.
Only You, You again,
always You.
You! You! You!
When I am gladdened—You.
When I am saddened—You.
Only You, You again,
always You.
You! You! You!
Sky is You. Earth is You.
You above. You below.
In every trend, at every end.
Only You, You again,
always You.
You! You! You!

He gave the Torah to His people. The Torah is given to *all* the people of Israel, even though, as the homily of the Four Children indicates, not all the people are equally receptive.

Four types. Four biblical verses (Deuteronomy 6:20; Exodus 12:26, 13:14, 13:8) merely mention children asking or being told about the Exodus. From these disparate verses the Rabbis created a framework for personalized pedagogic instruction. They predicated dissimilar dispositions and varying degrees of maturity, and counseled that the story of the Exodus should be geared to the attitude and age of the questioner. "The parent should teach each child on the level of the child's understanding" (*Pesaḥim* 116a).

38

The four children. The wicked son represents the element of sheer perversity, the desire to distance oneself from the whole exercise of reflecting on God's marvelous deliverances.

The wise son represents the ambition to know all that can legitimately be known, and this need has to be satisfied. The simple son represents the attitude of unquestioning faith, of unsophisticated surrender to the will of God.

Highest of all is the son who does not know how to ask, representing that stage of worship in which the worshipper is so overwhelmed by the divine that even the quest for knowledge becomes an intrusion and God is adored in a silence more eloquent than words.

The wise child. While the biblical verse reads *etkhem,* "you," this Haggadah follows the Jerusalem Talmud, and some texts of the *Mekhilta,* in its use of the word *otanu,* "us." This clarifies the difference between the wise child and the wicked child, for then the wise child explicitly includes himself in the community, while the wicked child conspicuously excludes himself.

The wicked child. The literal meaning of *hak-heh et shinav* is "set his teeth on edge" (by a physical blow). But it might be more effective to meet his contemptuous challenge with a trenchant retort.

The child who does not know. Noting that the word *at,* in the phrase *at p'tah lo,* consists of the first and last letters (*alef* and *tav*) of the Hebrew alphabet, Rabbi Ḥayim Halberstam of Zanz sees all the heavenly gates, from the highest to the lowest, opening to those who know that they do not know. And to these individuals, who temper wisdom with humility, divine insights are accordingly accorded.

Praised be He who is everywhere.
Praised be He.
Praised be He who gave the Torah to His people Israel.
Praised be He.

The Four Children

The Torah alludes to four types of children: one who is wise, and one who is wicked, one who is simple, and one who does not know how to ask.

What does the wise child ask? "What are the statutes, the laws and the ordinances which Adonai our God has commanded us?" (Deuteronomy 6:20). You should inform this child of all the laws of Pesaḥ, including the ruling that nothing should be eaten after the *afikomen.*

What does the wicked child ask? "What does this ritual mean to *you?*" (Exodus 12:26). To "you" and not to "him." Since he removes himself from the community by denying God's role in the Exodus, shake him by replying, "This is done because of what Adonai did for *me* when I went out of Mitzrayim" (Exodus 13:8). "For me." Not for him. Had he been there, he would not have been redeemed.

What does the simple child ask? "What is this all about?" You should tell him, "It was with a mighty hand that Adonai took us out of Mitzrayim, out of the house of bondage" (Exodus 13:14).

As for the child who does not know how to ask, you should open the discussion for him, as it is written, "And you shall explain to your child on that day, 'It is because of what Adonai did for me when I went free out of Mitzrayim'" (Exodus 13:8).

מתחלה

מִתְּחִלָּה עוֹבְדֵי עֲבוֹדָה זָרָה הָיוּ אֲבוֹתֵינוּ. וְעַכְשָׁו קֵרְבָנוּ הַמָּקוֹם לַעֲבוֹדָתוֹ, שֶׁנֶּאֱמַר: וַיֹּאמֶר יְהוֹשֻׁעַ אֶל כָּל הָעָם, כֹּה אָמַר יהוה אֱלֹהֵי יִשְׂרָאֵל: בְּעֵבֶר הַנָּהָר יָשְׁבוּ אֲבוֹתֵיכֶם מֵעוֹלָם, תֶּרַח אֲבִי אַבְרָהָם וַאֲבִי נָחוֹר. וַיַּעַבְדוּ אֱלֹהִים אֲחֵרִים. וָאֶקַּח אֶת אֲבִיכֶם, אֶת אַבְרָהָם, מֵעֵבֶר הַנָּהָר, וָאוֹלֵךְ אוֹתוֹ בְּכָל אֶרֶץ כְּנָעַן. וָאַרְבֶּה אֶת זַרְעוֹ, וָאֶתֶּן לוֹ אֶת יִצְחָק. וָאֶתֵּן לְיִצְחָק אֶת יַעֲקֹב וְאֶת עֵשָׂו. וָאֶתֵּן לְעֵשָׂו אֶת הַר שֵׂעִיר לָרֶשֶׁת אוֹתוֹ. וְיַעֲקֹב וּבָנָיו יָרְדוּ מִצְרָיִם.

בָּרוּךְ שׁוֹמֵר הַבְטָחָתוֹ לְיִשְׂרָאֵל. בָּרוּךְ הוּא. שֶׁהַקָּדוֹשׁ בָּרוּךְ הוּא חִשַּׁב אֶת הַקֵּץ לַעֲשׂוֹת כְּמָה שֶׁאָמַר לְאַבְרָהָם אָבִינוּ בִּבְרִית בֵּין הַבְּתָרִים, שֶׁנֶּאֱמַר: וַיֹּאמֶר לְאַבְרָם יָדֹעַ תֵּדַע כִּי גֵר יִהְיֶה זַרְעֲךָ בְּאֶרֶץ לֹא לָהֶם וַעֲבָדוּם וְעִנּוּ אֹתָם אַרְבַּע מֵאוֹת שָׁנָה, וְגַם אֶת הַגּוֹי אֲשֶׁר יַעֲבֹדוּ דָּן אָנֹכִי, וְאַחֲרֵי כֵן יֵצְאוּ בִּרְכֻשׁ גָּדוֹל.

Raise the cup of wine in thanksgiving.

וְהִיא שֶׁעָמְדָה לַאֲבוֹתֵינוּ וְלָנוּ, שֶׁלֹּא אֶחָד בִּלְבָד עָמַד עָלֵינוּ לְכַלּוֹתֵנוּ אֶלָּא שֶׁבְּכָל דּוֹר וָדוֹר עוֹמְדִים עָלֵינוּ לְכַלּוֹתֵנוּ, וְהַקָּדוֹשׁ בָּרוּךְ הוּא מַצִּילֵנוּ מִיָּדָם.

Replace the cup.

In the beginning. In the third century before the common era, Palestine was the scene of a major power-play between the Seleucids of Syria (Aram) and the Ptolemies of Egypt. These inimical forces each viewed the Hebrews from a highly partial perspective. In order to validate their claims to the land of the Hebrews, it suited the Seleucids to see them as descendants of Aram, while it pleased the Ptolemies to recall their Egyptian origin. When the Seleucids succeeded the Ptolemies, the priestly establishment, in deference to the delicate sensibilities of their overlords, deleted provocative passages in the Haggadah and, at that point, according to one historian, eliminated "We were slaves to Pharaoh" in favor of "In the beginning our ancestors served idols" and verses from the Book of Joshua. Interestingly enough, the Judean masses ignored this high-handed exercise in sacerdotal censorship, and continued to recite both passages, even as we still recite them to this day.

Our ancestors served idols. Key to our understanding of the Exodus is the duality of the rabbinic definition of slavery. It is defined as 1) subjugation of a people to another people, national enslavement, lack of political autonomy; and as 2) idolatry, because this is a practice that enslaves, i.e. robs human beings of their personal independence, depriving them of freedom of action, freedom of expression, freedom of worship.

Beyond the River. His descendants are called Hebrews (*Ivrim*) because Abraham came from beyond (*mei-ever*) the Euphrates.

I took your father. When Abraham left Aram Naharayim, he left everything behind. When the Israelites left Mitzrayim, they carried with them the mentality of slaves, remembering the fleshpots but forgetting the fetters.

The promise. "In the beginning is the end, and in the end is the beginning." Our history is pregnant with hope, alive with pledges yet to be redeemed. For God gave us His word, and His word endures forever. Prophet after prophet bore witness that it had been uttered and could never be revoked. "We base our belief in the promise of future redemption on the promise made when we were exiles in Mitzrayim, and God vowed that He would judge our oppressors and recompense us for all the humiliation and harassment that had been our portion. Frequently and in many places, He reminds us of the deliverance from Mitzrayim, and the assurance of ultimate redemption is implicit in these reminders. For this reason we submissively endure our sufferings, and wait patiently for Him to honor His pledge."

Four hundred years. There are indications that God intended to commute the sentence and to reprieve us ahead of time (after 210 years). In the phrase *hishev et ha-ketz* (literally, calculated the end) the numerical values of the letters in *ketz* add up to 190. So it is adduced that God figured on subtracting this number from the four hundred years, even as He prefigured the exile.

In the beginning

In the beginning our ancestors served idols, but then God embraced us so that we might serve Him, as it is written, "And Joshua said to the people, 'Thus says Adonai, God of Israel: Long, long ago your ancestors dwelt beyond the River Euphrates, Terah, the father of Abraham and the father of Nahor. They served other gods. But I took your father Abraham from beyond the River, and I led him through all the land of Canaan. I multiplied his descendants. I gave him Isaac, and to Isaac I gave Jacob and Esau, and to Esau I gave Mount Seir as his inheritance. But Jacob and his children went down to Mitzrayim'" (Joshua 24:2–4).

Praised be He who keeps His promise to Israel. Praised be He who foresaw both our enslavement and our redemption when He made the covenant with our father Abraham (Genesis 15). As it is written, "He said unto Abram: Know for certain that your offspring shall be strangers in a strange land, and shall be enslaved and afflicted for four hundred years. But know with equal certainty that I will judge the nation that enslaved them, and that afterwards they will leave with great substance'" (Genesis 15: 13–14).

Raise the cup of wine in thanksgiving.

It is this promise that has sustained our ancestors and us, for not just one enemy has arisen to destroy us; rather in every generation there are those who seek our destruction, but the Holy One, praised be He, saves us from their hands.

Replace the cup.

תורה ומדרש

We have reached the heart of the Haggadah. The following four verses, from the book of Deuteronomy, beginning Arami oved avi, supply a succinct synopsis of the history of the Exodus. (This passage was originally recited every Shavuot by pilgrims bringing their first fruits to the Temple in Jerusalem.) We are about to expand each phrase, to expound each thought, citing biblical chapter and verse to support and illustrate our explanations.

צֵא וּלְמַד: אֲרַמִּי אֹבֵד אָבִי וַיֵּרֶד מִצְרַיְמָה, וַיָּגָר שָׁם בִּמְתֵי מְעָט. וַיְהִי שָׁם לְגוֹי גָּדוֹל, עָצוּם וָרָב. וַיָּרֵעוּ אֹתָנוּ הַמִּצְרִים וַיְעַנּוּנוּ. וַיִּתְּנוּ עָלֵינוּ עֲבֹדָה קָשָׁה. וַנִּצְעַק אֶל יהוה אֱלֹהֵי אֲבֹתֵינוּ, וַיִּשְׁמַע יהוה אֶת קֹלֵנוּ, וַיַּרְא אֶת עָנְיֵנוּ וְאֶת עֲמָלֵנוּ וְאֶת לַחֲצֵנוּ. וַיּוֹצִאֵנוּ יהוה מִמִּצְרַיִם בְּיָד חֲזָקָה וּבִזְרֹעַ נְטוּיָה וּבְמֹרָא גָּדֹל וּבְאֹתוֹת וּבְמֹפְתִים.

אֲרַמִּי אֹבֵד אָבִי וַיֵּרֶד מִצְרַיְמָה, וַיָּגָר שָׁם בִּמְתֵי מְעָט. וַיְהִי שָׁם לְגוֹי גָּדוֹל, עָצוּם וָרָב.

אֲרַמִּי אֹבֵד אָבִי וַיֵּרֶד מִצְרַיְמָה. אָנוּס עַל פִּי הַדִּבּוּר, כְּמָה שֶׁנֶּאֱמַר: יָדֹעַ תֵּדַע כִּי גֵר יִהְיֶה זַרְעֲךָ בְּאֶרֶץ לֹא לָהֶם, וַעֲבָדוּם וְעִנּוּ אֹתָם אַרְבַּע מֵאוֹת שָׁנָה.

בִּמְתֵי מְעָט. כְּמָה שֶׁנֶּאֱמַר: בְּשִׁבְעִים נֶפֶשׁ יָרְדוּ אֲבֹתֶיךָ מִצְרַיְמָה וְעַתָּה שָׂמְךָ יהוה אֱלֹהֶיךָ כְּכוֹכְבֵי הַשָּׁמַיִם לָרֹב.

Midrash, from the Hebrew root *d-r-sh* meaning to seek, to inquire, can be described as a never-ending journey into inner space, a voyage of discovery, for untold treasures lie beyond the tantalizing reaches of the text. "The full meaning of the biblical words was not disclosed once and for all. Every hour another aspect is unveiled. The word was given once: the effort to understand it must go on forever. It is not enough to accept or even to carry out the commandments. To study, to examine, to explore the Torah is a form of worship, a supreme duty. For the Torah is an invitation to perceptivity, a call for *continuous* understanding." The following *midrashim* form a running commentary on the scriptural account of how Jacob's descendants became slaves in Mitzrayim and were redeemed from Mitzrayim.

A wandering Aramean. This is taken as a reference to the patriarch Jacob who, like his grandfather Abraham, lived for a while in Aram, the birthplace of his mother, Rebekah.

A wandering Aramean. An alternative interpretation of this verse construes the adjective *oved* (wandering) as the verb *ibbed* (would have destroyed). This reading identifies Laban (Jacob's uncle) as the Aramean in question, and terms him more iniquitous than Pharaoh. For while the latter plotted to kill the sons, Laban aimed at the extinction of all the Israelites.

Went down to Mitzrayim. It was at the effusive invitation of the reigning Pharaoh that Joseph brought his brothers to Goshen. "Come to me and I will give you the good of the land of Mitzrayim and you shall eat the fat of the land. . . . For all the good things of Mitzrayim are yours" (Genesis 45:18–20).

The divine word. Ha-dibbur means the word, speech, revelation. It is also one of the ninety-one Rabbinic synonyms for God.

Your offspring shall be strangers. "You shall not oppress a stranger, for you know how it feels to be a stranger, seeing that you yourselves were strangers in the land of Mitzrayim" (Exodus 23:9). "When a stranger resides with you in your land, you shall not wrong him. The stranger who dwells with you shall be to you as one of your citizens; you shall love him as yourself, for you were strangers in the land of Mitzrayim. I, Adonai, am your God" (Leviticus 19:33–34). The Torah contains no fewer than thirty-six variations on this theme. Commandment after commandment is coupled with the reminder that we who have experienced pain in Mitzrayim must be sensitive to the pain of others, that we who have experienced injustice must deal justly (and also generously) with our fellows. The social legislation of the Torah—its passionate concern for the welfare of the stranger, the underprivileged, the widow, the orphan—is bonded to this deeply implanted communal memory.

Torah and Midrash

We have reached the heart of the Haggadah. The following four verses, from the book of Deuteronomy, beginning Arami oved avi, supply a succinct synopsis of the history of the Exodus. (This passage was originally recited every Shavuot by pilgrims bringing their first fruits to the Temple in Jerusalem.) We are about to expand each phrase, to expound each thought, citing biblical chapter and verse to support and illustrate our explanations.

Consider these verses: My father was a wandering Aramean, and with just a few people he went down to Mitzrayim and sojourned there. And there he became a great nation, mighty and numerous. The Egyptians dealt harshly with us and oppressed us; and they imposed hard labor upon us. We cried out to Adonai, the God of our ancestors; and Adonai heard our plea and saw our affliction, our misery and our oppression. Then Adonai took us out of Mitzrayim with a mighty hand and an outstretched arm, with awesome power, with signs and with wonders (Deuteronomy 26:5–8).

"My father was a wandering Aramean, and with just a few people he went down to Mitzrayim and sojourned there. And there he became a great nation, mighty and numerous" (Deuteronomy 26:5).

My father was a wandering Aramean, and he went down to Mitzrayim. He was impelled, by force of the divine word, as it is written, "Know for a certainty that your offspring shall be strangers in a strange land and they shall be enslaved and afflicted for four hundred years" (Genesis 15:13).

With just a few people. As it is written, "Your ancestors went down to Mitzrayim with seventy persons in all, and now Adonai your God has made you as numerous as the stars in the sky" (Deuteronomy 10:22).

וַיָּגָר שָׁם. מְלַמֵּד שֶׁלֹּא יָרַד יַעֲקֹב אָבִינוּ לְהִשְׁתַּקֵּעַ בְּמִצְרַיִם אֶלָּא לָגוּר שָׁם, שֶׁנֶּאֱמַר: וַיֹּאמְרוּ אֶל פַּרְעֹה לָגוּר בָּאָרֶץ בָּאנוּ כִּי אֵין מִרְעֶה לַצֹּאן אֲשֶׁר לַעֲבָדֶיךָ כִּי כָבֵד הָרָעָב בְּאֶרֶץ כְּנָעַן, וְעַתָּה יֵשְׁבוּ נָא עֲבָדֶיךָ בְּאֶרֶץ גֹּשֶׁן.

וַיְהִי שָׁם לְגוֹי גָּדוֹל. מְלַמֵּד שֶׁהָיוּ יִשְׂרָאֵל מְצֻיָּנִים שָׁם, מְסֻמָּנִים בְּמִצְוֺת כְּגוֹי בִּפְנֵי עַצְמוֹ. לֹא נֶחְשְׁדוּ עַל הָעֲרָיוֹת, וְלֹא עַל לְשׁוֹן הָרָע. וְלֹא שִׁנּוּ אֶת שְׁמָם וְלֹא שִׁנּוּ אֶת לְשׁוֹנָם.

עָצוּם וָרָב. כְּמָה שֶׁנֶּאֱמַר: וּבְנֵי יִשְׂרָאֵל פָּרוּ וַיִּשְׁרְצוּ וַיִּרְבּוּ וַיַּעַצְמוּ בִּמְאֹד מְאֹד, וַתִּמָּלֵא הָאָרֶץ אֹתָם.

וַיָּרֵעוּ אֹתָנוּ הַמִּצְרִים וַיְעַנּוּנוּ, וַיִּתְּנוּ עָלֵינוּ עֲבֹדָה קָשָׁה.

וַיָּרֵעוּ אֹתָנוּ הַמִּצְרִים. כְּפוּיֵי טוֹבָה הָיוּ. וְשִׁלְּמוּ רָעָה תַּחַת הַטּוֹבָה שֶׁעָשָׂה לָהֶם יוֹסֵף, כְּמָה שֶׁנֶּאֱמַר: וַיָּקָם מֶלֶךְ חָדָשׁ עַל מִצְרָיִם אֲשֶׁר לֹא יָדַע אֶת יוֹסֵף. עָשָׂה אֶת עַצְמוֹ כְּאִלּוּ לֹא יָדַע אֶת יוֹסֵף.

דָּבָר אַחֵר: וַיָּרֵעוּ אֹתָנוּ הַמִּצְרִים. שֶׁעָשׂוּ אֹתָנוּ רָעִים, כְּמָה שֶׁנֶּאֱמַר: הִנֵּה עַם בְּנֵי יִשְׂרָאֵל רַב וְעָצוּם מִמֶּנּוּ. הָבָה נִתְחַכְּמָה לוֹ פֶּן יִרְבֶּה, וְהָיָה כִּי תִקְרֶאנָה מִלְחָמָה וְנוֹסַף גַּם הוּא עַל שֹׂנְאֵינוּ וְנִלְחַם בָּנוּ וְעָלָה מִן הָאָרֶץ.

Mitzrayim. The Hebrew word for Egypt occurs more than 700 times in the Bible. Only the name Israel occurs more frequently. Yet there is not a single derogatory reference to the Egyptians.

The Torah makes two things perfectly clear. The Israelites were bidden to abhor the abominations practiced in Mitzrayim ("You shall not copy the practices of the land," Leviticus 18:3). But with equal sternness they were cautioned against harboring a grudge against their onetime taskmasters. ("You shall not despise the Egyptians. Remember, you were once a sojourner in their land.") This is surely the most positive negative commandment ever written into a moral code.

Rashi's comment on this verse underlines the importance of hospitality — and of gratitude: "It is true that the Egyptians drowned our children in the Nile, but earlier, during the famine, they gave us refuge and made us welcome in their land."

The Egyptians dealt harshly with us. The word *va-yareiu* can mean "and they made us look bad." Until then, remembering Joseph with favor, the Egyptians were, for the most part, friendly and even grateful to the Israelites. So Pharaoh's first step was to sow the seeds of envy and distrust. He began by depicting the Israelites as potentially dangerous. Then he tried furtively to persuade the midwives to kill the Israelite children at birth. When this failed, he called openly upon the citizenry to implement his infanticidal design: "Pharaoh charged all his people, saying, 'Every boy that is born you shall throw into the Nile'" (Exodus 1:22). By then, Pharaoh's poisonous propaganda had taken effect, and the Egyptians were ready to collaborate in the programmed destruction of their former friends.

The Protocols of Pharaoh. The Israelites were loyal citizens, zealous in their duty to their adopted homeland. So we do not know what motivated Pharaoh to single them out for mistreatment, and deprive them of their civil rights. But we do know that despots through the ages have duplicated and refined his satanic strategy: causeless hatred fired by insidious innuendo, escalating into systematic persecution, mass expulsion and calculated genocide.

The Egyptians were ungrateful. By masterminding a food storage plan on a nation-wide scale during Mitzrayim's years of plenty, Joseph saved the whole population from starvation during the grievous famine that followed. But this counted for nothing when Pharaoh decided to persecute the Jews.

Too many for us. In the eyes of our detractors we loom larger and stronger than we really are. According to legend, the Israelites were outstanding for their valor and their heroism, qualities which they employed in the service of Mitzrayim. Yet when they rescued the country from defeat during a series of major wars, the Egyptians reacted with paranoid fear and suspicion.

They might join our enemies. With such seditious suppositions Pharaoh fomented friction among his gullible subjects. In the end, the Israelites left Mitzrayim aided by Mitzrayim's worst enemy—the Egyptians themselves.

And sojourned there. This teaches that our father Jacob did not go down to settle permanently in Mitzrayim but rather to sojourn there, as it is written, "And Jacob's sons said to Pharaoh, 'We have come to sojourn in this land, since there is no pasture for your servants' flock, for the famine in the land of Canaan is severe. Pray let your servants stay awhile in the land of Goshen'" (Genesis 47:4).

And there he became a great nation. This teaches that the Israelites became easily identifiable there. They became unique, recognized as a distinctive nation, through their observance of *mitzvot*. They were never suspected of unchastity or of slander; they did not change their names and they did not change their language.

Mighty and numerous. As it is written, "The Israelites were fruitful and prolific; they multiplied and increased greatly, so that the land was filled with them" (Exodus 1:7).

"The Egyptians dealt harshly with us and oppressed us; and they imposed hard labor upon us" (Deuteronomy 26:6).

The Egyptians dealt harshly with us. They were ungrateful, for they paid back in evil the kindnesses that Joseph had done for them, as it is written, "A new king arose over Mitzrayim who did not know Joseph" (Exodus 1:8). He acted as if he did not know about Joseph.

Another interpretation: The Egyptians dealt harshly with us. They made us appear to be bad, for it is written that Pharaoh said to his people, "Behold, the Israelites are too many and too mighty for us. Come, let us deal cunningly with them, lest they multiply, for then, in the event of war, they might join our enemies and fight against us and later leave our land" (Exodus 1:9–10).

וַיְעַנּוּנוּ. כְּמָה שֶׁנֶּאֱמַר: וַיָּשִׂימוּ עָלָיו שָׂרֵי מִסִּים לְמַעַן עַנֹּתוֹ בְּסִבְלֹתָם, וַיִּבֶן עָרֵי מִסְכְּנוֹת לְפַרְעֹה, אֶת פִּתֹם וְאֶת רַעַמְסֵס. וַיַּעֲבִדוּ מִצְרַיִם אֶת בְּנֵי יִשְׂרָאֵל בְּפָרֶךְ.

וַיִּתְּנוּ עָלֵינוּ עֲבֹדָה קָשָׁה. שֶׁהָיוּ מַחֲלִיפִין מְלֶאכֶת גָּדוֹל לְקָטָן וּמְלֶאכֶת קָטָן לְגָדוֹל, מְלֶאכֶת זָקֵן לְבָחוּר וּמְלֶאכֶת בָּחוּר לְזָקֵן. הֲרֵי זוֹ עֲבֹדָה שֶׁאֵין לָה קִצְבָה, שֶׁלֹּא רָצוּ לְשַׁעְבֵּד אוֹתָם בִּלְבַד אֶלָּא אַף לְדַכְּאָם.

וַנִּצְעַק אֶל יהוה אֱלֹהֵי אֲבֹתֵינוּ, וַיִּשְׁמַע יהוה אֶת קֹלֵנוּ, וַיַּרְא אֶת עָנְיֵנוּ וְאֶת עֲמָלֵנוּ וְאֶת לַחֲצֵנוּ.

וַנִּצְעַק אֶל יהוה. כְּמָה שֶׁנֶּאֱמַר: וַיְהִי בַיָּמִים הָרַבִּים הָהֵם וַיָּמָת מֶלֶךְ מִצְרַיִם, וַיֵּאָנְחוּ בְנֵי יִשְׂרָאֵל מִן הָעֲבֹדָה וַיִּזְעָקוּ, וַתַּעַל שַׁוְעָתָם אֶל הָאֱלֹהִים מִן הָעֲבֹדָה.

אֱלֹהֵי אֲבֹתֵינוּ. בִּזְכוּת אָבוֹת נִגְאֲלוּ מִמִּצְרַיִם, כְּמָה שֶׁנֶּאֱמַר: וַיִּשְׁמַע אֱלֹהִים אֶת נַאֲקָתָם, וַיִּזְכֹּר אֱלֹהִים אֶת בְּרִיתוֹ אֶת אַבְרָהָם אֶת יִצְחָק וְאֶת יַעֲקֹב.

וַיִּשְׁמַע יהוה אֶת קֹלֵנוּ. כְּמָה שֶׁנֶּאֱמַר: רָאֹה רָאִיתִי אֶת עֳנִי עַמִּי אֲשֶׁר בְּמִצְרָיִם וְאֶת צַעֲקָתָם שָׁמַעְתִּי מִפְּנֵי נֹגְשָׂיו, כִּי יָדַעְתִּי אֶת מַכְאֹבָיו. וָאֵרֵד לְהַצִּילוֹ מִיַּד מִצְרַיִם וּלְהַעֲלֹתוֹ מִן הָאָרֶץ הַהִיא. וְנֶאֱמַר: עִמּוֹ אָנֹכִי בְצָרָה. וְנֶאֱמַר: בְּכָל צָרָתָם לוֹ צָר.

וַיַּרְא. מָה רָאָה? שֶׁהָיוּ בְּנֵי יִשְׂרָאֵל מְרַחֲמִים זֶה עַל זֶה. הָיָה אֶחָד מֵהֶם מַשְׁלִים אֶת סְכוּם הַלְּבֵנִים שֶׁלּוֹ, וְהָיָה מְסַיֵּעַ לַחֲבֵרוֹ.

The Tree of Life and the Cult of Death. Why did the Egyptians regard the Israelites as a threat rather than a valuable source of manpower? Because these immigrants clung obdurately to their own language, their own values, their own invisible God. Fundamentally, this was a struggle between two cultures, between the Book of the Dead and the Tree of Life, between decadence and morality.

"When we compare the Egyptian attitude towards death with that of the Torah, we see in the latter what appears to be a deliberate aim to wean the Israelites from Egyptian superstition. On the one hand, there is not a word concerning reward and punishment in the Hereafter; on the other hand, there is rigorous proscription of all magic and sorcery, of sacrificing to the dead, as well as every form of alleged intercourse with the world of spirits. Israel's faith is a religion of *life*, not of death; a religion that declares man's humanity to man as the most acceptable form of adoration of the One God."

Ruthlessly (be-farekh). Playing on the Hebrew word, the Rabbis read it as "with a smooth tongue" (be-feh rakh). With fair words and the prospect of fair wages, the Israelites were tricked into forced labor. Enticement-entrapment. The honey and the sting. Our history is studded with unedifying examples of this treacherous tactic. From the soup-kitchen blandishments of missionaries to racist attempts to discredit Zionism, the onslaughts of our antagonists have often been cloaked in the tattered mantle of "humanitarianism" or the facile verbiage of pseudo-diplomacy.

The king died. With the death of the tyrant who had enslaved them, the Israelites hoped for the annulment of the evil decrees. When the new ruler renewed the edicts, they realized that the persecution was a matter of national policy. Despairingly, they appealed to God.

The Israelites cried out. To prevent them from mobilizing against their oppressors, the Israelites were forbidden to complain, even to each other. However, under cover of the national mourning for Pharaoh, the Israelites were able to express their anguish.

Their cry rose up. When there was a shortage of construction materials, the Egyptian overseers would seize the children of the laborers and bury them alive inside the walls of the buildings. The children wept within those terrible tombs. And God heard their weeping.

The merit of the fathers. Proxy piety? A talismanic crutch? Far from it. This peculiarly Jewish concept links parents and progeny in inter-generational harmony, a shared concern for bringing earth closer to heaven. The memory of saintly ancestors can serve, consciously or unconsciously, to guide, inspire and strengthen, sometimes saving us from ourselves.

What did God see? He saw people of the caliber of Amram, father of Miriam, Aaron and Moses. He saw that the Egyptians had weakened but not warped the moral fiber of the Israelites. He saw that His people deserved His compassion—because they showed compassion towards each other.

And oppressed us. As it is written, "So they set taskmasters over the Israelites to oppress them with forced labor; and they built store-cities for Pharaoh: Pithom and Raamses. . . . The Egyptians ruthlessly compelled the Israelites to toil with rigor" (Exodus 1:11, 13).

And they imposed hard labor upon us. They would impose a difficult task upon the weak and an easy task upon the strong, a light burden upon the young and a heavy burden upon the old. This was work without end and futile, for the Egyptians wanted not only to enslave them but also to break their spirit.

"We cried out to Adonai, the God of our ancestors; and Adonai heard our plea and saw our affliction, our misery, and our oppression" (Deuteronomy 26:7).

We cried out to Adonai. As it is written, "It came to pass in the course of time that the king of Mitzrayim died. The Israelites groaned under their burdens and cried out, and their cry to be free from bondage rose up to God" (Exodus 2:23).

The God of our ancestors. Because of the merit of our ancestors, we were redeemed from Mitzrayim. As it is written, "God heard their moaning, and recalled His covenant with Abraham, with Isaac and with Jacob" (Exodus 2:24).

And Adonai heard our plea. As it is written, "I have seen the affliction of My people in Mitzrayim, and I have heard their cry because of their taskmasters, and I know of their sufferings. And I have come down to deliver them out of the hands of the Egyptians, and to bring them out of that land" (Exodus 3:7–8). And it is written, "I shall be with Israel in trouble" (Psalms 91:15). And it is written, "In all their afflictions He was afflicted" (Isaiah 63:9).

And saw. What did He see? He saw that the Israelites had compassion for each other. When one of them finished his quota of bricks, he would help others.

אֶת עָנְיֵנוּ. זוֹ פְּרִישׁוּת דֶּרֶךְ אֶרֶץ. גָּזְרוּ עֲלֵיהֶם אֲנָשִׁים יָלִינוּ בַּשָּׂדֶה וְהַנָּשִׁים בָּעִיר, כְּדֵי לְמַעֲטָן בִּפְרִיָּה וּרְבִיָּה. וּנְשֵׁיהֶם מְחַמְּמוֹת לָהֶם חַמִּין וּמְבִיאוֹת לְבַעֲלֵיהֶן כָּל מַאֲכָל וּמִשְׁתֶּה, וּמְנַחֲמוֹת אֹתָם וְאוֹמְרוֹת: לְעוֹלָם לֹא מִשְׁתַּעְבְּדִין בָּנוּ, סוֹף הַקָּדוֹשׁ בָּרוּךְ הוּא גּוֹאֵל אֹתָנוּ. מִתּוֹךְ כָּךְ בָּאִים עֲלֵיהֶן וּפָרִים וְרָבִים. מִכָּאן שֶׁבִּזְכוּת נָשִׁים צִדְקָנִיּוֹת שֶׁהָיוּ בְּאוֹתוֹ הַדּוֹר נִגְאֲלוּ יִשְׂרָאֵל מִמִּצְרָיִם.

וְאֶת עֲמָלֵנוּ. אֵלוּ הַבָּנִים. שֶׁפַּרְעֹה גָּזַר: כָּל הַבֵּן הַיִּלּוֹד הַיְאֹרָה תַּשְׁלִיכֻהוּ וְכָל הַבַּת תְּחַיּוּן. הָיוּ יִשְׂרָאֵל מָלִים אֶת בְּנֵיהֶם בְּמִצְרָיִם. אָמְרוּ לָהֶם מִצְרִיִּים: לָמָה אַתֶּם מָלִים אוֹתָם, שֶׁלְּאַחַר שָׁעָה אָנוּ מַשְׁלִיכִים אֹתָם בַּנָּהָר? אָמְרוּ לָהֶם: אַף עַל פִּי כֵן נִמּוֹל אוֹתָם.

וְאֶת לַחֲצֵנוּ. זֶה הַדֹּחַק. שֶׁפַּרְעֹה גָּזַר: לֹא תֹאסִפוּן לָתֵת תֶּבֶן לָעָם לִלְבֹּן הַלְּבֵנִים כִּתְמוֹל שִׁלְשֹׁם. הֵם יֵלְכוּ וְקֹשְׁשׁוּ לָהֶם תֶּבֶן. הָיוּ בָּאִים הַמִּצְרִים וּמוֹנִים אֶת הַלְּבֵנִים וְנִמְצְאוּ חֲסֵרוֹת. וְשׁוֹטְרֵי יִשְׂרָאֵל לֹא הָיוּ מוֹסְרִים אֶת בְּנֵי יִשְׂרָאֵל בְּיַד הַמִּצְרִים. מָסְרוּ עַצְמָם עַל בְּנֵי יִשְׂרָאֵל וְסָבְלוּ מַכּוֹת כְּדֵי לְהָקֵל מֵעֲלֵיהֶם.

This refers to the enforced separation. One theory posits that the segregation was compulsory; a second theory suggests that it was voluntary. When Amram heard Pharaoh's fiat condemning newborn sons to death, he separated himself from his wife Yocheved. All the Israelite couples followed suit, whereupon Miriam remonstrated with her father, Amram. "Your conduct is more damaging than Pharaoh's mandate," she contended, "for Pharaoh sentenced only the male children, whereas you have pronounced sentence against all children." Amram found her argument convincing. He returned to his wife, and the other husbands were reunited with their spouses. Yocheved conceived and gave birth to Moses.

The merit of the mothers. Pharaoh's fatal mistake was his underestimation of the women. When the midwives to the Hebrew women, Shifra and Puah, refused to set expediency above conscience and refused to collaborate in the annihilation of their charges, the Israelite "resistance movement" was born. Despite the knowledge that they might be brutally bereft of their infants, the women of Israel continued to give birth, continued to bring sustenance and strength, courage and consolation to their disheartened husbands. Behind Moses, hero of the Exodus, stood heroic women: Yocheved, his mother; Miriam, who watched over her baby brother and contrived to have their mother appointed his nurse. And, in the greatest irony of all, an Egyptian princess, Pharaoh's own daughter, drew Moses from the Nile ... and became the instrument of Israel's redemption.

This refers to the drowning of the sons. Pharaoh's ultimate aim was the destruction of the Israelites, not their enslavement. If the Egyptians wanted slaves, why would they kill the children? History has proved that rational considerations are often irrelevant. Pharaoh's heirs, driven by a manic determination to destroy the Jews, have often pursued their monstrous objectives even when these became counterproductive, demonstrably detrimental to the economy of the "host country."

Every boy that is born you shall throw into the Nile. "Where the sin was committed the judgment takes place." Water became an agent of retribution. The first plague turned to blood all the waters of Mitzrayim, the rivers, the streams, the pools and the ponds that had "shed the blood" of little children. And, punished measure for measure, the Egyptians eventually came to a watery end in the Sea of Reeds.

This refers to the straw. At the first flickerings of insurrection, Pharaoh instituted harsher work-rules, designed to crush the Israelites' faith in Moses and in God. At first, the stratagem was effective. The hapless slaves accused Moses of making matters worse, of increasing rather than lightening their load.

The overseers suffered willingly. Later, when God said to Moses in the desert, "Gather seventy elders for Me" (Numbers 11:16), Moses replied, "I do not know who is worthy." God indicated that the Jewish overseers in Mitzrayim had proved their worth when they balked at mistreating their people, undertaking to suffer in their stead.

Our affliction. This refers to the enforced separation of husbands and wives. The Egyptians decreed that men should sleep in the field and women should sleep in the city, in order to decrease their offspring. The women, however, would bring warm food to their husbands, and comfort them, saying, "They shall not succeed in subjugating us. In the end, the Holy One will redeem us." Thus, in spite of the decree, they would be together and they did have children. Through the merit of the righteous women of that generation the Israelites were redeemed from Mitzrayim.

Our misery. This refers to the drowning of the sons, for Pharaoh decreed, "Every boy that is born you shall throw into the Nile, but you shall let every girl live" (Exodus 1:22). The Israelites would circumcise their sons in Mitzrayim. The Egyptians would ask, "Why do you insist upon circumcising them? In a little while we shall throw them into the river." The Israelites would respond, "Nevertheless we shall circumcise them."

And our oppression. This refers to the straw. For Pharaoh decreed, "You shall no longer provide the people with straw for making bricks; let them go and gather straw for themselves" (Exodus 5:7). Whenever the Egyptians counted the bricks and found the quota unfilled, the Israelite overseers refused to deliver their fellow Israelites to the Egyptians. Instead, they submitted themselves, and willingly suffered the punishment in order to lighten the ordeal of their fellow Israelites.

וַיּוֹצִאֵנוּ יְהוָה מִמִּצְרַיִם בְּיָד חֲזָקָה וּבִזְרֹעַ נְטוּיָה
וּבְמֹרָא גָּדֹל וּבְאֹתוֹת וּבְמֹפְתִים.

"Then Adonai took us out of Mitzrayim with a mighty hand and an outstretched arm, with awesome power, with signs and with wonders" (Deuteronomy 26:8).

וַיּוֹצִאֵנוּ יהוה מִמִּצְרָיִם. לֹא עַל יְדֵי מַלְאָךְ וְלֹא עַל יְדֵי שָׂרָף וְלֹא עַל יְדֵי שָׁלִיחַ, אֶלָּא הַקָּדוֹשׁ בָּרוּךְ הוּא בִּכְבוֹדוֹ וּבְעַצְמוֹ, שֶׁנֶּאֱמַר: וְעָבַרְתִּי בְאֶרֶץ מִצְרַיִם בַּלַּיְלָה הַזֶּה, וְהִכֵּיתִי כָל בְּכוֹר בְּאֶרֶץ מִצְרַיִם מֵאָדָם וְעַד בְּהֵמָה, וּבְכָל אֱלֹהֵי מִצְרַיִם אֶעֱשֶׂה שְׁפָטִים, אֲנִי יהוה.

וְעָבַרְתִּי בְאֶרֶץ מִצְרַיִם בַּלַּיְלָה הַזֶּה. אֲנִי וְלֹא מַלְאָךְ. וְהִכֵּיתִי כָל בְּכוֹר. אֲנִי וְלֹא שָׂרָף. וּבְכָל אֱלֹהֵי מִצְרַיִם אֶעֱשֶׂה שְׁפָטִים. אֲנִי וְלֹא הַשָּׁלִיחַ. אֲנִי יהוה. אֲנִי הוּא וְלֹא אַחֵר.

בְּיָד חֲזָקָה וּבִזְרֹעַ נְטוּיָה. כְּשֶׁמֵּרְרוּ הַמִּצְרִים אֶת חַיֵּי אֲבֹתֵינוּ, אָמַר הַקָּדוֹשׁ בָּרוּךְ הוּא: וְגָאַלְתִּי אֶתְכֶם, שֶׁנֶּאֱמַר: וְהוֹצֵאתִי אֶתְכֶם מִתַּחַת סִבְלֹת מִצְרַיִם וְהִצַּלְתִּי אֶתְכֶם מֵעֲבֹדָתָם וְגָאַלְתִּי אֶתְכֶם בִּזְרֹעַ נְטוּיָה וּבִשְׁפָטִים גְּדֹלִים. וְלָקַחְתִּי אֶתְכֶם לִי לְעָם וְהָיִיתִי לָכֶם לֵאלֹהִים, וִידַעְתֶּם כִּי אֲנִי יהוה אֱלֹהֵיכֶם.

וּבְמֹרָא גָּדוֹל. זֶה גִּלּוּי שְׁכִינָה, כְּמָה שֶׁנֶּאֱמַר: אוֹ הֲנִסָּה אֱלֹהִים לָבוֹא לָקַחַת לוֹ גוֹי מִקֶּרֶב גּוֹי, בְּמַסֹּת בְּאֹתֹת וּבְמוֹפְתִים וּבְמִלְחָמָה, וּבְיָד חֲזָקָה וּבִזְרֹעַ נְטוּיָה וּבְמוֹרָאִים גְּדֹלִים, כְּכֹל אֲשֶׁר עָשָׂה לָכֶם יהוה אֱלֹהֵיכֶם בְּמִצְרַיִם לְעֵינֶיךָ.

וּבְאֹתוֹת. זֶה הַמַּטֶּה, כְּמָה שֶׁנֶּאֱמַר: וְאֶת הַמַּטֶּה הַזֶּה תִּקַּח בְּיָדֶךָ אֲשֶׁר תַּעֲשֶׂה בּוֹ אֶת הָאֹתֹת.

דָּבָר אַחֵר: וּבְאֹתוֹת. אֵלּוּ מִצְוֹת יהוה. שֶׁהֵם אוֹת לְעוֹלָם שֶׁהוּא אֵל מַצִּיל וּמוֹשִׁיעַ, וְזִכָּרוֹן בְּכָל דּוֹר וָדוֹר לַבְּרִית שֶׁבֵּין הַקָּדוֹשׁ בָּרוּךְ הוּא לְבֵין עַמּוֹ, כְּמָה שֶׁנֶּאֱמַר: וְהָיָה לְךָ לְאוֹת עַל יָדְךָ וּלְזִכָּרוֹן בֵּין עֵינֶיךָ, לְמַעַן תִּהְיֶה תּוֹרַת יהוה בְּפִיךָ, כִּי בְּיָד חֲזָקָה הוֹצִאֲךָ יהוה מִמִּצְרָיִם.

I and no other. Why does the Haggadah pass over the architect of the Exodus, the father of the prophets, that "colossus among the great figures of humanity," our teacher *Moshe Rabbenu?* By this daring omission, the Rabbis dramatized God's direct intervention in history, demonstrating that He alone had extricated the Israelites from Mitzrayim. At the same time, the Rabbis forestalled the emergence of a personality cult. No other leader in Jewish history can rank with Moses "whom Adonai knew face to face," but this towering figure inspires reverence, not deification.

A mighty hand. The redemption from Mitzrayim and the final redemption are part of the same process, "of the mighty hand and outstretched arm," which began in Mitzrayim, and is evident in all of history. Moses and Elijah belong to the same redemptive act; one represents its beginning and the other its culmination, so that together they fulfill its purpose. The spirit of Israel is attuned to the hum of the redemptive process, to the sound waves of its labors which will end only with coming of the days of the Messiah.

You shall know that I am Adonai. God actually executed the judgment of death Himself. Obviously, the Holy One, blessed be He, could have given the Israelites the power to avenge themselves upon the Egyptians, but instead He took great pains to remove Israel from any participation in the vengeance upon the evildoers. For that reason, the darkest hour was designated . . . and the Israelites were warned not to step outside their houses at midnight—all this in order to detach them completely from the deeds of destruction.

Four in Folklore. This is a night of counting, as well as recounting, and the number four figures repeatedly in the evening scenario. There are four questions, four children, four kinds of food and four cups of wine. Wherefore so many fours? Because, it is said, of the four qualities that helped Israel to survive in Mitzrayim, because of the four meritorious matriarchs, because of the four banners the Israelites carried in the wilderness, because of the four exiles we endured, and because of the four nights of watching. *The Book of Remembrance* records four nights of revelation: the night He revealed Himself to create the universe, the night He revealed Himself to make the covenant with Abraham, the night He revealed Himself to rescue us from Mitzrayim, and the night (still to come) when He will reveal Himself to redeem us for good.

I will take you out. This verse contains four expressions of redemption: "I will free you," "I will deliver you," "I will redeem you," and "I will take you to be My people." The Four Cups that we drink tonight represent these four steps to freedom.

A sign and a symbol. This is a reference to the *tefillin* worn on forehead and arm during weekday morning worship. "Master of the universe, when a Jew drops his *tefillin* on the floor, he hastily picks them up and kisses them." So testifies Rabbi Levi Yitzḥak of Berditchev in one of his famous colloquies with God. "Your *tefillin*, Your people Israel, have lain on the ground for nearly two thousand years. Why do You let them lie there, trodden underfoot? When will You gather up Your *tefillin* and embrace them?"

Then Adonai took us out of Mitzrayim. Not by an angel. Nor by a seraph. Nor by a messenger. Rather, the Holy One Himself, in His glory, as it is written, "For that night I will pass through Mitzrayim, and I will strike down every firstborn in Mitzrayim, both man and beast; and on all the gods of Mitzrayim I will execute judgments. I am Adonai" (Exodus 12:12).

"I will pass through Mitzrayim" — I and not an angel. "And I will strike down every firstborn" — I and not a seraph. "And on all the gods of Mitzrayim I will execute judgments" — I and not a messenger. "I am Adonai" — I and no other.

With a mighty hand and an outstretched arm. When the Egyptians made the life of our ancestors bitter, the Holy One said, "I will redeem them," as it is written, "I will free you from the burdens of the Egyptians, and I will deliver you from their bondage. I will redeem you with an outstretched arm and through extraordinary judgments. I will take you to be My people, and I will be your God. And you shall know that I, Adonai, am your God" (Exodus 6:6–7).

With awesome power. This refers to divine revelation, as it is written, "Has God ever taken for Himself one nation from the midst of another, with prodigious acts, with signs and wonders, with war, with a mighty hand and an outstretched arm, and with awesome power, as Adonai your God did for you in Mitzrayim before your eyes?" (Deuteronomy 4:34).

With signs. This refers to the staff, as it is written, "And in your hand take this staff with which you shall perform the signs" (Exodus 4:17).

Another interpretation: With signs. This refers to God's commandments. For they are an eternal sign that God saves and redeems, and a remembrance for all generations of the covenant between the Holy One and His people. Thus it is written, "And this shall serve you as a sign on your hand, and as a symbol on your forehead — in order that the teachings of Adonai may be in your mouth — that with a mighty hand Adonai freed you from Mitzrayim" (Exodus 13:9).

וּבְמֹפְתִים. אֵלוּ הַמַּכּוֹת,
כְּמָה שֶׁנֶּאֱמַר: וְנָתַתִּי מוֹפְתִים
בַּשָּׁמַיִם וּבָאָרֶץ:
דָּם וָאֵשׁ וְתִימְרוֹת עָשָׁן.

And with wonders. This refers to the plagues, as it is written, "And I will show you wonders in the heavens and on earth, blood and fire and columns of smoke" (Joel 3:3).

דָּם צְפַרְדֵּעַ כִּנִּים עָרוֹב
דֶּבֶר שְׁחִין בָּרָד אַרְבֶּה
חֹשֶׁךְ מַכַּת בְּכוֹרוֹת

רַבִּי יְהוּדָה הָיָה נוֹתֵן בָּהֶם סִימָן.
דְּצַ"ךְ עַדַ"שׁ בְּאַחַ"ב.

WHY do we remove ten drops of wine from our cups? We glory in our liberation, but we do not gloat over our fallen foes. When the waters of the Sea of Reeds engulfed the Egyptians, the ministering angels began to sing praises. But God silenced them, saying, "My children perish. Cease your songs!" So we celebrate with less than a full heart, with less than a full cup.

These are the ten plagues. Why were there plagues? Why ten plagues? And why these ten plagues? The *makkot* can be classified as punitive strikes; they can also be viewed as opportunities for repentance. Each chastisement was announced in advance, providing Pharaoh with ten face-saving occasions to relent and to relinquish his stranglehold on the Israelites. But Pharaoh could not, would not see the error of his ways, and his hard heart was hardened. While God could undoubtedly have rescued the Israelites by other means, the plagues were necessary ploys in a cosmological confrontation. "The contest was far more than a dramatic humiliation of the unrepentant and infatuated tyrant. It was nothing less than a judgment on all the gods of Mitzrayim (Exodus 12:12). The plagues fell on the principal divinities that were worshipped since time immemorial in the Nile Valley. The river was a god; it became loathsome to its worshippers. The frog was venerated as a sign of fruitfulness, and it was turned into a horror. The cattle — the sacred ram, the sacred goat, the sacred bull — were all smitten. The sacred beetle became a torment to those who had put their trust in its divinity. When we add the plague of darkness which showed the eclipse of Ra, the sun-god, we see that we have here a contrast between the God of Israel, the Master of the universe, and the senseless gods of a senile civilization."

Rabbi Judah made an acrostic. Why did he do this? Perhaps he used this euphemistic contraction because he did not like to linger on the subject. Or perhaps the mnemonic was intended to help us remember the *ten* plagues in the order recorded in the Book of Exodus (since different versions occur in different texts, Psalms 78 and 105, for instance).

According to midrashic legend, this acrostic pre-dated Rabbi Judah. For it was engraved upon the staff of Moses, the staff that was created on the eve of the very first Shabbat. With this staff, Moses performed the "signs," in Pharaoh's court and in the wilderness.

Did the Holy One bring the plagues upon the Egyptians, or did the Egyptians bring the plagues upon themselves? Environmentalists contend that pollution is a man-made problem. Do the air and seas pollute themselves? Moreover, there is a moral, or more accurately, *im*moral dimension to the wanton contamination of the elements. In the same way that Noah's contemporaries called forth the flood, in the same way that the sinful cities of Sodom and Gomorrah caused fire and brimstone to consume them, so the Egyptians, by their depraved and licentious lifestyle, tainted their environment, blighted their own lives. The first nine plagues can be construed as extreme manifestations of natural phenomena.

עֶשֶׂר מַכּוֹת הֵבִיא הַקָּדוֹשׁ בָּרוּךְ הוּא עַל הַמִּצְרִים בְּמִצְרַיִם וְאֵלּוּ הֵן:

These are the ten plagues which the Holy One brought upon the Egyptians:

At the mention of each plague, remove a drop of wine from your cup.

BLOOD FROGS VERMIN BEASTS
CATTLE PLAGUE BOILS HAIL LOCUSTS
DARKNESS   DEATH OF THE FIRSTBORN

Rabbi Judah made them into an acrostic:

D'TZaKH   ADaSH   B'AHaB.

דַּיֵּנוּ

כַּמָּה מַעֲלוֹת טוֹבוֹת לַמָּקוֹם עָלֵינוּ.

אִלּוּ הוֹצִיאָנוּ מִמִּצְרַיִם
וְלֹא עָשָׂה בָהֶם שְׁפָטִים,   דַּיֵּנוּ.

אִלּוּ עָשָׂה בָהֶם שְׁפָטִים
וְלֹא עָשָׂה בֵאלֹהֵיהֶם,   דַּיֵּנוּ.

אִלּוּ עָשָׂה בֵאלֹהֵיהֶם
וְלֹא קָרַע לָנוּ אֶת הַיָּם,   דַּיֵּנוּ.

אִלּוּ קָרַע לָנוּ אֶת הַיָּם
וְלֹא הֶעֱבִירָנוּ בְּתוֹכוֹ בֶּחָרָבָה,   דַּיֵּנוּ.

אִלּוּ הֶעֱבִירָנוּ בְּתוֹכוֹ בֶּחָרָבָה
וְלֹא סִפֵּק צָרְכֵּנוּ בַּמִּדְבָּר אַרְבָּעִים שָׁנָה,   דַּיֵּנוּ.

אִלּוּ סִפֵּק צָרְכֵּנוּ בַּמִּדְבָּר אַרְבָּעִים שָׁנָה
וְלֹא הֶאֱכִילָנוּ אֶת הַמָּן,   דַּיֵּנוּ.

אִלּוּ הֶאֱכִילָנוּ אֶת הַמָּן
וְלֹא נָתַן לָנוּ אֶת הַשַּׁבָּת,   דַּיֵּנוּ.

אִלּוּ נָתַן לָנוּ אֶת הַשַּׁבָּת
וְלֹא קֵרְבָנוּ לִפְנֵי הַר סִינַי,   דַּיֵּנוּ.

אִלּוּ קֵרְבָנוּ לִפְנֵי הַר סִינַי
וְלֹא נָתַן לָנוּ אֶת הַתּוֹרָה,   דַּיֵּנוּ.

אִלּוּ נָתַן לָנוּ אֶת הַתּוֹרָה
וְלֹא הִכְנִיסָנוּ לְאֶרֶץ יִשְׂרָאֵל,   דַּיֵּנוּ.

אִלּוּ הִכְנִיסָנוּ לְאֶרֶץ יִשְׂרָאֵל
וְלֹא בָנָה לָנוּ אֶת בֵּית הַבְּחִירָה,   דַּיֵּנוּ.

עַל אַחַת כַּמָּה וְכַמָּה טוֹבָה כְפוּלָה וּמְכֻפֶּלֶת לַמָּקוֹם עָלֵינוּ. שֶׁכֵּן עָשָׂה כָּל הַנִּפְלָאוֹת הָאֵלֶּה מִיצִיאַת מִצְרַיִם עַד בִּנְיַן בֵּית הַבְּחִירָה.

He divided the sea for us. The Bible records quite matter-of-factly that a strong east wind caused the sea to recede. But harking back to pre-creation chaos, a curious old myth tells of wild howling waters, the waters above and the waters below, so enamored with each other that they flouted the divine directive to separate, clinging together in amorous embrace until they were torn apart. Then the upper waters (the mists and clouds) were gathered into the firmament, and the lower waters (the rivers and seas) subsided into their appointed places. Although they could have been trounced for insubordination, the mutinous waters received a conditional pardon. The condition? They were contracted to aid the Exodus, parting in order to permit safe conduct for the Israelites.

He led us across on dry land. Intricate, colorful embroideries embellish the crossing which took place in the presence of the matriarchs and the patriarchs who rejoiced at the prodigious feats wrought on behalf of their chastened children. And not only did the Israelites walk dryshod between towering walls of water, but sweet springs sprang up to slake their thirst and luscious fruits appeared to still their hunger.

He took care of us. An earthly employer requires his workers to minister to him. The Master of the universe appointed us His servitors, then tended us tenderly, taking care of all our needs.

He gave us the Torah. When the Torah came into the world, say the Rabbis, freedom came into the world.

He took care of us in the desert. What is the purpose of life's trials and tribulations? Are we being punished for transgressions? Or do we suffer so that we may be recompensed? It is possible that obstacles are set before us as character-building exercises, framed to foster our growth. Maimonides supplies this case in point: our wanderings through "the great and dreadful wilderness wherein were serpents, fiery serpents, and scorpions and thirsty grounds," were not a penance but a preparation. The Israelites would not have been able to cope with the conquest of Canaan had they not endured the disciplines of the desert.

He gave us the Torah. We all stood at the foot of Mount Sinai and we all heard the divine pronouncement. But what exactly did we hear? All of the ten Commandments? The first two Commandments? Or only the first word, the first sound, the aleph of "I" (Anokhi)? If we accept the radical premise, advanced by Rabbi Mendel of Rymanov, that we heard the "immense aleph" alone, then what we heard was the preparation for communication. For aleph is the source of articulate sound, encompassing the whole alphabet and all human discourse. It remained for Moses and his heirs to translate the sound, to interpret and communicate the substance. "The Torah contains, in actuality or in embryo, all knowledge, all wisdom," say the sages. Everything our teachers have taught us through the ages was already made known to Moses at Sinai. Continuity of revelation is maintained. And our prayers are addressed to God who gives us the Torah every day, in the hope that every day we will receive it anew and fulfill it anew.

DAYYENU (It would have been enough)

With measured and mounting jubilation, this lilting litany chronicles an extraordinary progression. It tells how God in His lovingkindness raised us, step by step, from the degradation of slavery to the heights of freedom as His chosen people. We express our thankfulness for every beneficent act, and we delight in the Godly design that plotted our path—via Sinai—to our Promised Land.

How many acts of kindness God has performed for us!

Had He taken us out of Mitzrayim without carrying out judgments against the Egyptians — *Dayyenu.*

Had he carried out judgments against the Egyptians without vanquishing their gods — *Dayyenu.*

Had He vanquished their gods without dividing the sea for us — *Dayyenu.*

Had He divided the sea for us without leading us across on dry land — *Dayyenu.*

Had He led us across on dry land without taking care of us for forty years in the desert — *Dayyenu.*

Had He taken care of us for forty years in the desert without feeding us manna — *Dayyenu.*

Had He fed us manna without giving us Shabbat — *Dayyenu.*

Had He given us Shabbat without bringing us to Mount Sinai — *Dayyenu.*

Had He brought us to Mount Sinai without giving us the Torah — *Dayyenu.*

Had He given us the Torah without leading us to the Land of Israel — *Dayyenu.*

Had He led us to the Land of Israel without building the Temple for us — *Dayyenu.*

How manifold and miraculous are the great deeds that our God has performed for us, from taking us out of Mitzrayim to building the Temple.

וַיֻּגַּד לְמֶלֶךְ מִצְרַיִם כִּי בָרַח הָעָם, וַיֵּהָפֵךְ לְבַב פַּרְעֹה וַעֲבָדָיו אֶל הָעָם וַיֹּאמְרוּ: מַה זֹּאת עָשִׂינוּ כִּי שִׁלַּחְנוּ אֶת יִשְׂרָאֵל מֵעָבְדֵנוּ? וַיִּרְדְּפוּ מִצְרַיִם אַחֲרֵיהֶם וַיַּשִּׂיגוּ אוֹתָם חֹנִים עַל הַיָּם. וַיָּבֹאוּ בְנֵי יִשְׂרָאֵל בְּתוֹךְ הַיָּם בַּיַּבָּשָׁה, וְהַמַּיִם לָהֶם חוֹמָה מִימִינָם וּמִשְּׂמֹאלָם. וַיִּרְדְּפוּ מִצְרַיִם וַיָּבֹאוּ אַחֲרֵיהֶם, כֹּל סוּס פַּרְעֹה רִכְבּוֹ וּפָרָשָׁיו אֶל תּוֹךְ הַיָּם. וַיָּשֻׁבוּ הַמַּיִם וַיְכַסּוּ אֶת הָרֶכֶב וְאֶת הַפָּרָשִׁים. לְכֹל חֵיל פַּרְעֹה הַבָּאִים אַחֲרֵיהֶם בַּיָּם, לֹא נִשְׁאַר בָּהֶם עַד אֶחָד. וַתִּקַּח מִרְיָם הַנְּבִיאָה אֲחוֹת אַהֲרֹן אֶת הַתֹּף בְּיָדָהּ, וַתֵּצֶאןָ כָּל הַנָּשִׁים אַחֲרֶיהָ בְּתֻפִּים וּבִמְחֹלֹת. וַתַּעַן לָהֶם מִרְיָם: שִׁירוּ לַיהוה כִּי גָאֹה גָּאָה, סוּס וְרֹכְבוֹ רָמָה בַיָּם.

The Israelites went into the sea. The odds were three hundred to one against the fleeing Israelites, but neither the charging chariots of Pharaoh nor the necromantic machinations of all Mitzrayim's arch-magicians could harm them. Escorted by a pillar of light by night and by a pillar of cloud by day, they decamped and sallied forth to safety.

Walls of water. So spectacular were the sights that accompanied this crossing that a servantmaid at the Sea of Reeds beheld greater wonders than Ezekiel in his loftiest visions. Yet noting that Psalm 136 praises God with equal fervor for "sundering the Sea" and for "giving food to all flesh," the Rabbis conclude that both acts are equally fantastic. Earning a living, day in, day out, is little short of a miracle. Every morsel of bread is a demonstration of benign divine providence.

Not a single one remained. Pharaoh himself, according to legend, did not perish in the Sea of Reeds. He repented, and was delivered from the depths. Later he was appointed king of Nineveh. When that city's impending doom was announced by the reluctant prophet Jonah, the king led his people in fasting and penitential prayers. And Nineveh was spared. Now, when tyrants gravitate to their eternal unrest, the reformed Pharaoh greets them with hindsight's vexatious wisdom: "Why did you not profit from my example?"

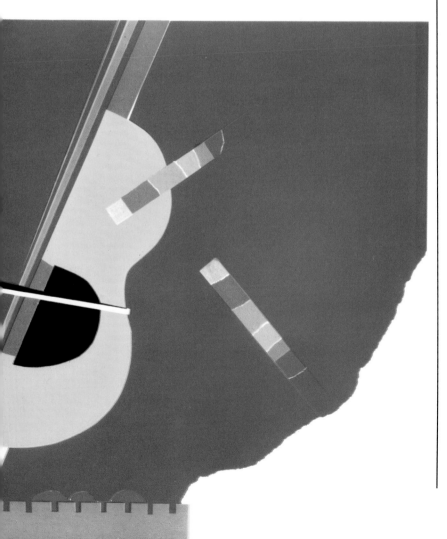

The miracle. There is no doubt about one miracle. This wandering tribe, in many respects indistinguishable from numberless nomadic communities, grasped and proclaimed an idea of which all the genius of Greece and all the power of Rome were incapable. There was to be only one God, a universal God, a God of all nations, a just God.

Miriam the prophet. "I sent before you Moses, Aaron and Miriam" (Micah 6:4). Miriam is ranked with her brothers as one of the liberators of ancient Israel. Many *midrashim* tell of her resourcefulness, her leadership, her outspokenness, her wisdom and her beauty. Because of her merits, runs one Miriam myth, the Israelites were blessed with fresh sweet water all the days of her life. Throughout those forty years in the droughty desert, the wanderers were accompanied by "Miriam's well," a movable, miraculous well. This peripatetic oasis was the wellspring of refreshment, fragrance, lush greenery—and some very tall tales.

The women went out with timbrels. Timbrels? How did timbrels happen to materialize on the windswept shores of the Sea of Reeds? How did the women happen to have timbrels in their hand luggage? Ask yourself what you would take if you were required, at short notice, to leave your home for a journey of unspecified duration to an unidentified destination. Household goods? Clothing? Family treasures? The women of ancient Israel, in such a predicament, had enough imagination and enough faith to pack musical instruments. They knew that God would perform miracles for His people, and they wanted the wherewithal to celebrate. In such homey details, we glimpse the valor and the values of Israel's frontier women.

When they were told that the people had fled, Pharaoh and his courtiers had a change of heart and said, "What have we done, releasing Israel from our service?" The Egyptians gave chase, and overtook them encamped by the sea. The Israelites went into the sea on dry ground, the waters forming a wall for them on their right and on their left. The Egyptians pursued the Israelites into the sea, all of Pharaoh's horses, chariots and horsemen. Then the waters turned back and covered all the horses, chariots and horsemen. Of Pharaoh's entire army not a single one remained. Then Miriam the prophet, Aaron's sister, took a timbrel in her hand, and all the women went out after her with timbrels and with dances. And Miriam chanted for them, "Sing to Adonai, for He has triumphed gloriously; horse and rider has He hurled into the sea" (Exodus 14:5, 9, 22, 23, 28; 15:20–21).

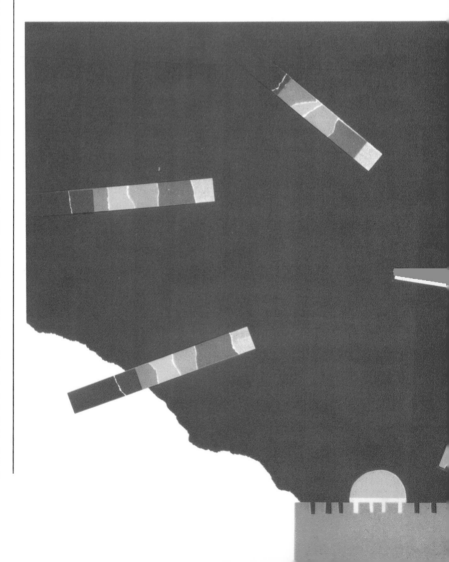

רַבָּן גַּמְלִיאֵל הָיָה אוֹמֵר: כָּל שֶׁלֹּא אָמַר שְׁלשָׁה דְבָרִים אֵלּוּ בַּפֶּסַח לֹא יָצָא יְדֵי חוֹבָתוֹ, וְאֵלּוּ הֵן: פֶּסַח, מַצָּה, וּמָרוֹר.

We remember the Pesaḥ offering eaten in Temple times, as we recite:

פֶּסַח, שֶׁהָיוּ אֲבוֹתֵינוּ אוֹכְלִים בִּזְמַן שֶׁבֵּית הַמִּקְדָּשׁ הָיָה קַיָּם, עַל שׁוּם מָה? עַל שׁוּם שֶׁפָּסַח הַקָּדוֹשׁ בָּרוּךְ הוּא עַל בָּתֵּי אֲבוֹתֵינוּ בְּמִצְרַיִם, שֶׁנֶּאֱמַר: וַאֲמַרְתֶּם זֶבַח פֶּסַח הוּא לַיהוה, אֲשֶׁר פָּסַח עַל בָּתֵּי בְנֵי יִשְׂרָאֵל בְּמִצְרַיִם, בְּנָגְפּוֹ אֶת מִצְרַיִם, וְאֶת בָּתֵּינוּ הִצִּיל.

מַצָּה זוֹ שֶׁאָנוּ אוֹכְלִים, עַל שׁוּם מָה? עַל שׁוּם שֶׁלֹּא הִסְפִּיק בְּצֵקָם שֶׁל אֲבוֹתֵינוּ לְהַחֲמִיץ, עַד שֶׁנִּגְלָה עֲלֵיהֶם מֶלֶךְ מַלְכֵי הַמְּלָכִים הַקָּדוֹשׁ בָּרוּךְ הוּא וּגְאָלָם, שֶׁנֶּאֱמַר: וַיֹּאפוּ אֶת הַבָּצֵק אֲשֶׁר הוֹצִיאוּ מִמִּצְרַיִם עֻגֹת מַצּוֹת, כִּי לֹא חָמֵץ. כִּי גֹרְשׁוּ מִמִּצְרַיִם וְלֹא יָכְלוּ לְהִתְמַהְמֵהַּ, וְגַם צֵדָה לֹא עָשׂוּ לָהֶם.

מָרוֹר זֶה שֶׁאָנוּ אוֹכְלִים, עַל שׁוּם מָה? עַל שׁוּם שֶׁמֵּרְרוּ הַמִּצְרִים אֶת חַיֵּי אֲבוֹתֵינוּ בְּמִצְרַיִם, שֶׁנֶּאֱמַר: וַיְמָרְרוּ אֶת חַיֵּיהֶם בַּעֲבֹדָה קָשָׁה, בְּחֹמֶר וּבִלְבֵנִים וּבְכָל עֲבֹדָה בַּשָּׂדֶה, אֵת כָּל עֲבֹדָתָם אֲשֶׁר עָבְדוּ בָהֶם בְּפָרֶךְ.

בְּכָל דּוֹר וָדוֹר חַיָּב אָדָם לִרְאוֹת אֶת עַצְמוֹ כְּאִלּוּ הוּא יָצָא מִמִּצְרַיִם, שֶׁנֶּאֱמַר: וְהִגַּדְתָּ לְבִנְךָ בַּיּוֹם הַהוּא לֵאמֹר: בַּעֲבוּר זֶה עָשָׂה יהוה לִי בְּצֵאתִי מִמִּצְרַיִם. לֹא אֶת אֲבוֹתֵינוּ בִּלְבָד גָּאַל הַקָּדוֹשׁ בָּרוּךְ הוּא, אֶלָּא אַף אוֹתָנוּ גָּאַל עִמָּהֶם, שֶׁנֶּאֱמַר: וְאוֹתָנוּ הוֹצִיא מִשָּׁם לְמַעַן הָבִיא אֹתָנוּ לָתֶת לָנוּ אֶת הָאָרֶץ אֲשֶׁר נִשְׁבַּע לַאֲבֹתֵינוּ.

Pesaḥ. Matzah. Maror. When the Temple was destroyed, the task of the Rabbis was to prove that the spirit of Pesaḥ was indestructible. They reinforced the loaded symbolism of the Seder—the authenticated signs of God's involvement in the fortunes and misfortunes of His people. Even as He had rescued us once, plucking us from the very midst of another nation and bearing us "on eagles' wings" unto Himself, so He would rescue us again and again.

Explaining Pesaḥ. An unwonted emphasis on explanations distinguishes this night from all other nights. Judaism stresses deeds, not dogma. "We shall do and we shall obey, *naaseh v'nishma,*" affirm the Israelites at Sinai. Yet, in discussions over the relative importance of study and practice, Rabbi Akiva speaks for the majority of his colleagues when he insists that study is more important, since learning about *mitzvot* leads to performance of *mitzvot*. At the Seder we discuss the *matzah* and the *maror*. And we eat the *matzah* and the *maror*. Thus we rehearse for ourselves and for our children the lessons of Pesaḥ, and we internalize these lessons.

Pesaḥ. Risking dire reprisals from those who held the lamb sacred, the Israelites meticulously prepared the *Pesaḥ* offering and meticulously observed that first Pesaḥ in Mitzrayim. It must have been a night of vigilance and unease as, tragically, so many Pesaḥ evenings were to be. In times of danger and duress, with bloodthirsty mobs howling at the door, amid bullets and bombs, Jews strove to observe the Seder ritual. Among honored survivors of the Holocaust are scraps of paper, makeshift Haggadot, written by hand, written by heart, written within sight of the smoking crematoria.

Matzah. The bread of affliction suddenly became the bread of redemption. The very abruptness of the deliverance reminds us that help can come when it is least expected, even when the sword is poised to descend, even when arsenals (and nuclear warheads) are readied against us, even beyond the eleventh hour.

Nor had they prepared other provisions. How many of us would pack a few handfuls of dough and without further ado leave our homes for an undetermined destination? This, as Rashi points out, is exactly what our ancestors did in Mitzrayim. Even though they were to stray and stumble during the tortuous travels that lay ahead, the downtrodden slaves had been capable of a consummate act of faith. "I remember the affection of your youth, the love of your espousals, how you followed Me into the wilderness, into a land that was not sown" (Jeremiah 2:2).

Maror. This symbol has never lost its pungency for it has never been in short supply. And this serves to sharpen the point: the bitterness of servitude gives way to the sweetness of freedom, and *maror* is replaced by the many-splendored taste of manna.

In each generation. In an ideal sense, all Israel went forth out of Mitzrayim, and all Israel stood before Sinai; and all Israel moved through darkness to the presence of God, in the wake of a pillar of fire. Whenever trumpets sound in history, they sound for all ages; and when the bell tolls, the echo lives on forever.... The Haggadah is the script of a living drama, not the record of a dead event, and when Jews recite it, they are performing an act not of remembrance but of personal identification in the here and now.

Rabban Gamliel would say: "Those who have not explained three things during the Seder have not fulfilled their obligation. These three things are: the Pesaḥ offering, matzah and maror."

We remember the Pesaḥ offering eaten in Temple times, as we recite:

Pesaḥ: Why did our ancestors eat the *Pesaḥ* offering at their Seder? As a reminder that the Holy One, praised be He, passed over the Israelite dwellings in Mitzrayim, as it is written: "You shall say, 'It is the *Pesaḥ* offering to Adonai, because He passed over the houses of the Israelites in Mitzrayim when He smote the Egyptians and spared our homes'" (Exodus 12:27).

Matzah: Why do we eat it? To remind ourselves that even before the dough of our ancestors had time to rise, the supreme King of kings, the Holy One, praised be He, revealed Himself and redeemed them, as it is written: "And they baked the dough which they had brought from Mitzrayim into unleavened cakes (*matzot*); it did not rise since they were hurried out of Mitzrayim, and they could not delay, nor had they prepared other provisions for themselves" (Exodus 12:39).

Maror: Why do we eat it? To remind ourselves that, as it is written, the Egyptians in Mitzrayim "embittered the lives of our ancestors with hard labor, in mortar and in brick, and in every manner of drudgery in the field; and worked them ruthlessly in all their labor" (Exodus 1:14).

In each generation, every individual should feel as though he or she had actually been redeemed from Mitzrayim, as it is said: "You shall tell your children on that day, saying, 'It is because of what Adonai did for me when I went free out of Mitzrayim'" (Exodus 13:8). For the Holy One redeemed not only our ancestors; He redeemed us with them, as it is said, "He brought us out of there, so that He might bring us to the land He promised our ancestors" (Deuteronomy 6:23).

לְפִיכָךְ אֲנַחְנוּ חַיָּבִים לְהוֹדוֹת לְהַלֵּל לְשַׁבֵּחַ לְפָאֵר
לְרוֹמֵם לְהַדֵּר לְבָרֵךְ לְעַלֵּה וּלְקַלֵּס לְמִי שֶׁעָשָׂה
לַאֲבוֹתֵינוּ וְלָנוּ אֶת כָּל הַנִּסִּים הָאֵלּוּ. הוֹצִיאָנוּ
מֵעַבְדוּת לְחֵרוּת
מִיָּגוֹן לְשִׂמְחָה
מֵאֵבֶל לְיוֹם טוֹב
וּמֵאֲפֵלָה לְאוֹר גָּדוֹל
וּמִשִּׁעְבּוּד לִגְאֻלָּה
וְנֹאמַר לְפָנָיו שִׁירָה חֲדָשָׁה.
הַלְלוּיָהּ.

הַלְלוּ אֶת שֵׁם יהוה.	הַלְלוּיָהּ, הַלְלוּ עַבְדֵי יהוה
מֵעַתָּה וְעַד עוֹלָם.	יְהִי שֵׁם יהוה מְבֹרָךְ
מְהֻלָּל שֵׁם יהוה.	מִמִּזְרַח שֶׁמֶשׁ עַד מְבוֹאוֹ
עַל הַשָּׁמַיִם כְּבוֹדוֹ.	רָם עַל כָּל גּוֹיִם יהוה
הַמַּגְבִּיהִי לָשָׁבֶת.	מִי כַּיהוה אֱלֹהֵינוּ
בַּשָּׁמַיִם וּבָאָרֶץ.	הַמַּשְׁפִּילִי לִרְאוֹת
מֵאַשְׁפֹּת יָרִים אֶבְיוֹן.	מְקִימִי מֵעָפָר דָּל
עִם נְדִיבֵי עַמּוֹ.	לְהוֹשִׁיבִי עִם נְדִיבִים
אֵם הַבָּנִים שְׂמֵחָה. הַלְלוּיָהּ.	מוֹשִׁיבִי עֲקֶרֶת הַבַּיִת

All these miracles. During the Six-Day War, when Israel was once more beleaguered, outnumbered, imperiled, while the world once more adopted a wary non-interventionist pose, it seemed to Jews everywhere, inter-denominational differences submerged in shared anxiety, that only a miracle could save the small Jewish State. "When the Israeli victory came, and with such suddenness, there was among Jews, for a moment, a sense of the genuine presence of God in history once again. . . . Before the Temple's Western Wall in Jerusalem even Jewish agnostics prayed first and rationalized it later."

From enslavement to redemption. It is not often that an individual wants to be reminded of his humble beginnings; but that a nation in ancient times should glory in having been held in bondage by another nation is certainly an unrepeated phenomenon. Yet in the consciousness of the Jewish people the bondage in which their ancestors were held in Mitzrayim has been an ever-present memory, held vividly and related vitally to the entire context of their life. There is only one explanation. . . . The remembrance serves as a means of signalizing the unique character of the God whom Israel worships. With Israel's serfdom in Mitzrayim as background, Israel's God stands forth more sharply and luminously as the Redeemer of the oppressed, as the Liberator of the enslaved, as the Defender of the weak against the strong.

From darkness to light. The deliverance from Mitzrayim is important only because it paved the way to Sinai—that is, to Israel's voluntary acceptance of its special and distinctive mission; and the Seder narrative relates how Israel moved progressively from darkness to light, from the ignorance and shame of idolatry to the consciousness and glory of its high adventure.

From slavery to freedom. And from Auschwitz to Entebbe in a single generation.

Halleluyah. The "Egyptian Hallel" (Psalms 113 to 118) is one of the oldest sections of the Haggadah. These psalms were chanted by the Levites in the Temple during the Pesaḥ ritual. According to the Rabbis, these same psalms were chanted by the Israelites at the Sea of Reeds, the scene of the deliverance.

Sing praises, servants of Adonai. All forms of servitude result in sadness. Only the service of the Creator brings joy to the heart.

Servants? "Since we long ago, my noble friends, resolved never to be servants to the Romans nor to any other than to God Himself who alone is the true and just Ruler of mankind, the time has now come that obligates us to make that resolution true in practice." So spoke Eleazer ben Jair to the defenders of Masada in the year 73 C.E., according to the stirring docu-drama outlined by Josephus. "Let us die before we become slaves under our enemies and let us go out of the world, together with our wives and our children, in a state of freedom." For seven years a few hundred zealots had held at bay the panoplied legions of Imperial Rome. When defeat became inevitable, they chose death by their own hands rather than dishonor.

The happy mother. Jeremiah painted Jerusalem as a desolate widow, and the community of Israel is often depicted as a grieving woman, childless or bereft. Yet the generation that has witnessed the liberation of Jerusalem, the Holy City made whole, wholly ours again, at one with itself and with its loved ones, has reason to believe that it is witnessing redemptive rays. Rachel still weeps for her children, but she no longer refuses to be comforted.

Lift the cup of wine and recite:

Therefore, we must revere, exalt, extol, acclaim, adore and glorify God who performed all these miracles for our ancestors and for us. He took us
> from slavery to freedom
> from despair to joy
> from mourning to celebration
> from darkness to light
> from enslavement to redemption
and we sing before Him a new song. Halleluyah!

Replace the cup.

Halleluyah! Praise Adonai.
Sing praises, you servants of Adonai.

> Let Adonai be praised now and always.

From east to west, praised is Adonai.

> He is exalted above all nations,
> His glory extends beyond the heavens.

Who is like Adonai our God, enthroned on high,
concerned with all below in heaven and on earth?

> He lifts the poor out of the dust,
> He raises the needy from despair,

He seats them with the powerful,
with the powerful of His people.

> He settles a barren woman in her home,
> a mother happy with her children. Halleluyah!

(Psalm 113)

בֵּית יַעֲקֹב מֵעַם לֹעֵז.
יִשְׂרָאֵל מַמְשְׁלוֹתָיו.
הַיַּרְדֵּן יִסֹּב לְאָחוֹר.
גְּבָעוֹת כִּבְנֵי צֹאן.
הַיַּרְדֵּן תִּסֹּב לְאָחוֹר.
גְּבָעוֹת כִּבְנֵי צֹאן.
מִלִּפְנֵי אֱלוֹהַּ יַעֲקֹב.
חַלָּמִישׁ לְמַעְיְנוֹ מָיִם.

בְּצֵאת יִשְׂרָאֵל מִמִּצְרָיִם
הָיְתָה יְהוּדָה לְקָדְשׁוֹ
הַיָּם רָאָה וַיָּנֹס
הֶהָרִים רָקְדוּ כְאֵילִים
מַה לְךָ הַיָּם כִּי תָנוּס
הֶהָרִים תִּרְקְדוּ כְאֵילִים
מִלִּפְנֵי אָדוֹן חוּלִי אָרֶץ
הַהֹפְכִי הַצוּר אֲגַם מָיִם

Lift the cup of wine and recite.

בָּרוּךְ אַתָּה יהוה אֱלֹהֵינוּ מֶלֶךְ הָעוֹלָם אֲשֶׁר גְּאָלָנוּ
וְגָאַל אֶת אֲבוֹתֵינוּ מִמִּצְרַיִם, וְהִגִּיעָנוּ לַלַּיְלָה הַזֶּה
לֶאֱכָל בּוֹ מַצָּה וּמָרוֹר. כֵּן יהוה אֱלֹהֵינוּ וֵאלֹהֵי
אֲבוֹתֵינוּ, יַגִּיעֵנוּ לְמוֹעֲדִים וְלִרְגָלִים אֲחֵרִים הַבָּאִים
לִקְרָאתֵנוּ לְשָׁלוֹם, שְׂמֵחִים בְּבִנְיַן עִירֶךָ, וְשָׂשִׂים
בַּעֲבוֹדָתֶךָ. וְנוֹדֶה לְךָ שִׁיר חָדָשׁ עַל גְּאֻלָּתֵנוּ וְעַל
פְּדוּת נַפְשֵׁנוּ. בָּרוּךְ אַתָּה יהוה גָּאַל יִשְׂרָאֵל.

כּוֹס שֵׁנִי

Reflection:

הִנְנִי מוּכָן/מוּכָנָה וּמְזֻמָּן/וּמְזֻמֶּנֶת לְקַיֵּם מִצְוַת כּוֹס שֵׁנִי שֶׁהוּא
כְּנֶגֶד בְּשׂוֹרַת הַיְשׁוּעָה שֶׁאָמַר הַקָּדוֹשׁ בָּרוּךְ הוּא לְיִשְׂרָאֵל:
וְהִצַּלְתִּי אֶתְכֶם מֵעֲבוֹדָתָם.

בָּרוּךְ אַתָּה יהוה אֱלֹהֵינוּ מֶלֶךְ הָעוֹלָם בּוֹרֵא פְּרִי
הַגָּפֶן.

Drink the wine while reclining.

When Israel left. Although they had lived for so many years among people of alien and abhorrent values, Israel left Mitzrayim as Israel, with its identity intact and its commitment to God reaffirmed for all eternity.

When the House of Jacob left. We are still in the process of leaving. "Every day," says Rabbi Israel of Kozhenitz, "we must free ourselves from Mitzrayim."

His domain. Since the Hebrew word means literally domains or spheres of dominion, the use of the plural form could connote recognition of the pluralistic nature of the Jewish people, united in its allegiance to God and His Torah yet characterized by infinite diversity. God guides each individual, each household, each grouping, even as He maps the course of the entire nation and the entire world.

O sea, why did you flee? The seas, the mountains, the rivers, the hills — all reacted to an earth-shattering act of God, as the God of Jacob took for Himself the most powerless of peoples in order to demonstrate through Israel His power and His presence in history. Amid seismic birth-pangs, Israel was born.

He turns rock into pools of water. Serfs are emancipated. The lowly are uplifted. And cold, granite hearts can warm to the word of God. Is anything impossible for Him who laid the foundations of the earth, who bound the chains of the Pleiades and loosed the bands of Orion?

Rebuilding Jerusalem. The restoration of Zion began on the day of its destruction. The land was rebuilt in time long before it was restored in space. We have been rebuilding it daily for nearly two thousand years.

A new song. We are engaged in what is probably the oldest ceremony of its kind, a ceremony with a virtually unbroken tradition of observance for well over three millennia. Yet there is nothing routine about this ritual, nothing perfunctory about our performance. Those who dwell fervently on the weighty minutiae of the Exodus will be found worthy of dwelling in the presence of the *Sh'khinah* in the world to come, since "rejoicing brings forth rejoicing; and the joy of Israel causes the Holy One Himself to be joyful.... All this terrestrial rejoicing increases the power of Adonai and His hosts in the regions above, just as an earthly king gains in stature when his subjects broadcast his fame far and wide."

When Israel left the land of Mitzrayim,
when the House of Jacob left alien people,

Judah became His holy one, Israel His domain.

The sea fled at the sight, the Jordan retreated.

Mountains leaped like rams, hills skipped like lambs.

O sea, why did you flee? Jordan, why did you retreat?

Mountains, why leap like rams, and hills like lambs?

Even the earth trembled at the presence of Adonai,
at the presence of Jacob's God

Who turns rock into pools of water,
flint into fountains.

(Psalm 114)

Lift the cup of wine and recite:

Praised are You, Adonai our God, King of the universe who has redeemed us and our ancestors from Mitzrayim, who has brought us to this night when we eat *matzah* and *maror*. Adonai, our God and God of our ancestors, enable us to celebrate in peace other holy days and festivals, joyful in the rebuilding of Your city Jerusalem and joyful in Your service. We will sing a new song of thanks for our redemption and for our spiritual liberation. Praised are You, Adonai, redeemer of the people Israel.

The Second Cup

Reflection:

I am ready to fulfill the commandment of drinking the second of the Four Cups. This recalls God's promise of redemption to the people Israel, as it says, "I will deliver you from bondage" (Exodus 6:6).

Praised are You, Adonai our God, King of the universe who creates the fruit of the vine.

Drink the wine while reclining.

Wash your hands and recite:

בָּרוּךְ אַתָּה יהוה אֱלֹהֵינוּ מֶלֶךְ הָעוֹלָם אֲשֶׁר קִדְּשָׁנוּ בְּמִצְוֹתָיו וְצִוָּנוּ עַל נְטִילַת יָדָיִם.

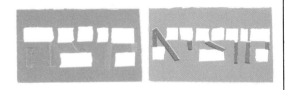

Lift the three matzot and recite:

בָּרוּךְ אַתָּה יהוה אֱלֹהֵינוּ מֶלֶךְ הָעוֹלָם הַמּוֹצִיא לֶחֶם מִן הָאָרֶץ.

בָּרוּךְ אַתָּה יהוה אֱלֹהֵינוּ מֶלֶךְ הָעוֹלָם אֲשֶׁר קִדְּשָׁנוּ בְּמִצְוֹתָיו וְצִוָּנוּ עַל אֲכִילַת מַצָּה.

Eat the matzah while reclining.

HOW: Using a pitcher or a cup, pour water over each hand, two or three times. Then recite the blessing.

WHY: The priests in the Temple would wash their hands before approaching the altar. Similarly, we wash our hands at this stage in order to approach the table with clean hands and a pure heart, so that we may sanctify the act of eating.

You have sanctified us. Enoch was a cobbler, hardly the most spiritual of occupations. Yet legend has it that with every stitch of his awl, when he sewed the uppers to the lowers, he welded heaven to earth. It is in our power to transmute ordinary into extraordinary, secular into sacred. For every desire, every impulse, every deed — waking, washing, working, eating — is sublimated and sanctified, when performed for the sake of heaven.

Washing our hands. The literal meaning of *netilah* is 'lifting.' So this word is used either because we raise our hands when we pour water over them, or because of the verse, "Lift up your hands to the Sanctuary and bless Adonai" (Psalms 134:2).

The ritual. Today we have no Temple in Jerusalem, no altar there, no sacrifices, no priests. But every home can be a Temple, every table an altar, every meal a sacrifice, every Jew a priest. And eating, a mechanical animal function, can be transformed into an elaborate ritual full of mystery and meaning.

HOW: Lift the three *matzot* (including the broken middle *matzah* remaining from *yaḥatz*) and recite the customary blessing over bread and the blessing over the *matzah*. Then divide the top *matzah* and/or the middle *matzah* among the participants. Eat some *matzah* while reclining.

ADDITIONAL NOTES: (a) The bottom *matzah* is reserved for *korekh* and should not be eaten to fulfill the *mitzvah* of *matzah*. (b) Since there is disagreement over whether this blessing is said over the broken middle *matzah* ("the bread of affliction") or the unbroken top *matzah*, some people eat a piece of each. (c) To fulfill the *mitzvah* of *matzah* and *maror*, the minimum amount to be eaten is a *ke-zayit*, the size of an olive.

Rohtzah

Wash your hands and recite:

Praised are You, Adonai our God, King of the universe who has sanctified our lives through His commandments, and commanded us to perform the ritual washing of our hands.

Motzi Matzah

Lift the three matzot and recite:

Praised are You, Adonai our God, King of the universe who brings forth bread from the earth.

Praised are You, Adonai our God, King of the universe who has sanctified our lives through His commandments, commanding us to partake of *matzah*.

Eat the matzah while reclining.

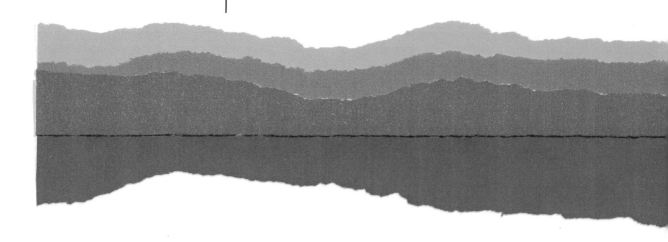

Dip some maror in ḥaroset and recite:

בָּרוּךְ אַתָּה יהוה אֱלֹהֵינוּ מֶלֶךְ הָעוֹלָם אֲשֶׁר קִדְּשָׁנוּ בְּמִצְוֹתָיו וְצִוָּנוּ עַל אֲכִילַת מָרוֹר.

Eat the maror without reclining.

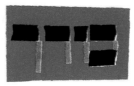

Sandwich some maror between two pieces of the bottom matzah and recite:

זֵכֶר לְמִקְדָּשׁ כְּהִלֵּל. כֵּן עָשָׂה הִלֵּל בִּזְמַן שֶׁבֵּית הַמִּקְדָּשׁ הָיָה קַיָּם. הָיָה כּוֹרֵךְ מַצָּה וּמָרוֹר וְאוֹכֵל בְּיַחַד, לְקַיֵּם מַה שֶׁנֶּאֱמַר: עַל מַצּוֹת וּמְרֹרִים יֹאכְלֻהוּ.

WHY: A variety of reasons, picturesque and poignant, are suggested for the inclusion of ḥaroset with the *maror*. (This is the second dipping.)

In color and texture, ḥaroset resembles the mortar that we were forced to make as slaves.

Its sweetness modifies the bitterness of the *maror*. But perhaps ḥaroset is more than a palatable palliative. Perhaps it is an expression of Jewish optimism, of the belief that the direst disaster has a redeeming feature. Thus one sanguine sage declares that the Messiah was born on the day that the Temple was destroyed.

The apples in ḥaroset also remind us that, according to rabbinic legend, our mothers in Mitzrayim would give birth beneath the benevolent boughs of sheltering apple trees. And there they would hide their infants in an unavailing bid to protect them from Egyptians, who would seek out the newborn Israelites and drown them. But God dispatched guardian angels to comfort the lorn women and watch over the little ones.

The ingredients of ḥaroset are related to the aromatic items mentioned in various verses of the Song of Songs which, according to tradition, is recited during Pesaḥ. Moreover, since Adam and Eve were permitted to take with them cinnamon and spices of that ilk when they were exiled from Eden, we can even trace in ḥaroset a hint of Paradise Lost.

Matzah, maror. Why do we eat *matzah* first and *maror* next, even though we suffered long before we were set free? Rabbi Simḥa Bunam of Pshiskhah explains: "As long as there was no prospect of release, the Israelites did not feel the full extent of their enslavement. But as soon as Moses spoke to them of freedom, they awoke to the bitterness of their lot."

WHY: According to Hillel, *matzah* and *maror* and the *Pesaḥ* offering were eaten together in a sandwich during Temple times. According to other authorities, the items were eaten one at a time. Today, in deference to Hillel, we eat a *matzah-maror* sandwich after we have fulfilled the *mitzvot* of *matzah* and of *maror* by eating each separately.

After the destruction of the Temple, the Rabbis emphasized that we were not eating a substitute for the *Pesaḥ* offering. Many people do not eat roasted meat during the meal because the *Pesaḥ* offering was roasted, and such points of similarity should be avoided.

Matzah, maror. This combination of *maror* and *matzah* has been called, by Philo, a moral migration from wickedness to virtue. Repentant sinners at first brood bitterly (*maror*) over their past misdeeds. Then *matzah*, the healing food, brings them to humility and contentment.

Maror

Dip some maror in ḥaroset and recite:

Praised are You, Adonai our God, King of the universe who has sanctified our lives through His commandments, commanding us to eat *maror.*

Eat the maror without reclining.

Korekh

Sandwich some maror between two pieces of the bottom matzah and recite:

This is a reminder of the Temple and a reminder of the practice of Hillel. While the Temple was in existence, Hillel would make a sandwich of the *Pesaḥ* offering, with *matzah* and *maror,* and eat all three together, in fulfillment of the verse, "with *matzot* and *maror* they shall eat it" (Numbers 9:11).

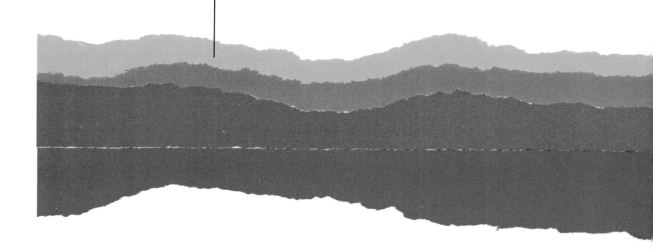

שולחן עורך

The festive meal. Tonight's meal, with its unusual setting and its unusual ingredients, is itself an occasion for festive rejoicing. In fact, since *Hallel* psalms are said before and after it, some commentators consider this meal to be part of *Hallel*—a palpable act of praise.

Beginning with eggs. It is customary to begin the meal with eggs dipped in salt water. Adding spice to the feast of freedom is the fact that we are free to select our own interpretations for its sundry symbols, interpretations factual or fanciful. For instance, why do we eat eggs? Perhaps because eggs are associated with mourning. (It cannot be simply a calendrical quirk that the fast commemorating the destruction of the Temple, *Tisha b'Av*, always occurs on the same day of the week as the first night of Pesaḥ.) Yet eggs do not merely conjure up a mournful memory. They also symbolize life, birth, fertility, regeneration.

HOW: The afikomen is distributed among the participants and eaten while reclining.

WHY: Because its significance was primarily symbolic, the *Pesaḥ* offering was eaten at the end of the meal when people were no longer hungry. In remembrance of this, we eat the *afikomen* at the end of our meal. The meaning of the Greek word *afikomen* is unclear. It probably means either dessert or the practice of going reveling from house to house after the Seder (*Pesaḥim* 119b). The Rabbis disallowed both postprandial partying (hardly compatible with the solemnity of the evening) and eating after the *Pesaḥ* offering (so that its flavor might linger). Today nothing is eaten or drunk after the *afikomen* (except for the third and fourth cups of wine).

Tzafun. The hiddenness of the *afikomen* intimates to us that the miracle of the Exodus was a preparation for future acts of redemption which are still hidden from us. The Exodus from Mitzrayim did not result in complete salvation. Every generation must contribute towards achievement of the final redemption.

Yaḥatz, the breaking of the middle *matzah*, is a silent, reflective act wherein part of the *matzah* is concealed to be searched out before the blessings that conclude the meal may be recited.

It is the larger piece of the middle *matzah* that is concealed. For more is hidden than is revealed. Within us, individually and collectively, there are prayers to be fulfilled, promises to be redeemed. We are, like the broken *matzah*, incomplete. Our children, in their searching, are extensions of our explorations.

We prepared for Pesaḥ in the night, searching for the hidden *ḥametz*; we end the Seder in the night, searching for the hidden *matzah*. To know there is concealment is to know that we must work for revealment, for completion. As with *yaḥatz*, so with eating the *afikomen*, no benediction is uttered, no word is spoken, for this is wordless discovery.

Shulḥan Orekh

The meal is served.

Tzafun

At the conclusion of the meal, eat the afikomen while reclining.

Fill the Third Cup.
For the short version of the blessings after the meal, Birkat Hamazon,
see page 88. Conclude with the Third Cup (page 92). On Shabbat and
festivals, Psalm 126, shir hama'alot, is the prologue to Birkat Hamazon.

The invitation. "If three people have eaten at one table without uttering words of Torah, it is as though they had worshipped idols." So says Rabbi Shimon bar Yoḥai. "But when three people eat together and engage in holy table-talk, it is as though they have eaten at God's table" (*Avot* 3:4). We began the evening by inviting fellow Jews to join us at our celebration. Now we invite our companions, a quorum of three or more, to join us in thanksgiving. The formula for this invitation, *zimmun*, which is found in the Mishnah (*Berakhot* 7:3), derives from the verse, "O magnify Adonai with me, and let us exalt His name together" (Psalms 34:4). Since prayer is so personal, why this emphasis on liturgical togetherness? And how is it humanly possible for us to "magnify" Him whose greatness defies measure? Our duty, our destiny, is to serve Him both as individuals and as a community. Furthermore, Creator and creation are interdependent. By serving His purpose here on earth, we exalt His name. God needs us — our good deeds, our living testimony — even as we need Him.

שִׁיר הַמַּעֲלוֹת. בְּשׁוּב יהוה אֶת שִׁיבַת צִיּוֹן הָיִינוּ כְּחֹלְמִים. אָז יִמָּלֵא שְׂחוֹק פִּינוּ וּלְשׁוֹנֵנוּ רִנָּה. אָז יֹאמְרוּ בַגּוֹיִם הִגְדִּיל יהוה לַעֲשׂוֹת עִם אֵלֶּה. הִגְדִּיל יהוה לַעֲשׂוֹת עִמָּנוּ, הָיִינוּ שְׂמֵחִים. שׁוּבָה יהוה אֶת שְׁבִיתֵנוּ כַּאֲפִיקִים בַּנֶּגֶב. הַזֹּרְעִים בְּדִמְעָה בְּרִנָּה יִקְצֹרוּ. הָלוֹךְ יֵלֵךְ וּבָכֹה, נֹשֵׂא מֶשֶׁךְ הַזָּרַע, בֹּא יָבֹא בְרִנָּה, נֹשֵׂא אֲלֻמֹּתָיו.

When three or more adults have eaten together, one of them formally invites the others to join in these blessings. (When ten or more are present, the words in parentheses are added.)

The leader:

רַבּוֹתַי נְבָרֵךְ.

The others respond:

יְהִי שֵׁם יהוה מְבֹרָךְ מֵעַתָּה וְעַד עוֹלָם.

The leader continues:

יְהִי שֵׁם יהוה מְבֹרָךְ מֵעַתָּה וְעַד עוֹלָם.
בִּרְשׁוּת רַבּוֹתַי, נְבָרֵךְ (אֱלֹהֵינוּ) שֶׁאָכַלְנוּ מִשֶּׁלּוֹ.

Matzah and morality. We can fulfill our obligation to eat *matzah* only by using grain that can easily become *hametz.* From this we learn that we cannot fulfill our obligations to God solely through Torah study and prayer. We must also serve God through our daily chores—in the way we eat, the way we earn our living, the way we conduct our affairs. It is possible to eat forbidden foods, to be dishonest, to indulge in unlawful activities. But when we perform routine actions in the right spirit, then we have truly served God. We have not allowed the *matzah* to become *hametz.*

Let us praise Him. This is the blessing that our father Abraham, most hospitable of hosts, taught his guests. After he had fed and refreshed them, he would urge them to direct their thanks not to him but to Adonai, the Provider of all.

Barekh

Fill the Third Cup.
For the short version of the blessings after the meal, Birkat Hamazon, see page 89. Conclude with the Third Cup (page 93). On Shabbat and festivals, Psalm 126, shir hama'alot, is the prologue to Birkat Hamazon.

When Adonai brought us back from exile to Zion, it was like a dream. Then our mouths were filled with laughter, joyous song was on our tongues. Then it was said among the nations: "Adonai has done great things for them." Great things indeed He did for us; therefore we rejoiced. Bring us back, Adonai, as You bring streams back to Israel's desert soil. Those who sow in tears shall reap in joy. He who goes his way in sadness, bearing his sack of seed, will yet come home in gladness, bearing ample sheaves of grain (Psalm 126).

When three or more adults have eaten together, one of them formally invites the others to join in these blessings. (When ten or more are present, the words in parentheses are added.)

The leader:

Friends, let us give thanks.

Rabotai n'varekh.

The others respond:

May Adonai be praised, now and forever.

Yehi shem adonai m'vorakh mei-attah v'ad olam.

The leader continues:

May Adonai be praised, now and forever.
With your consent, friends, let us praise (our God) the One whose food we have eaten.

Yehi shem adonai m'vorakh mei-attah v'ad olam.
Bir'shut rabotai, n'varekh (eloheinu) she'akhalnu mishelo.

The others respond:

בָּרוּךְ (אֱלֹהֵינוּ) שֶׁאָכַלְנוּ מִשֶּׁלּוֹ וּבְטוּבוֹ חָיִינוּ.

The leader continues:

בָּרוּךְ (אֱלֹהֵינוּ) שֶׁאָכַלְנוּ מִשֶּׁלּוֹ וּבְטוּבוֹ חָיִינוּ.

All together:

בָּרוּךְ הוּא וּבָרוּךְ שְׁמוֹ.

בָּרוּךְ אַתָּה יהוה אֱלֹהֵינוּ מֶלֶךְ הָעוֹלָם, הַזָּן אֶת הָעוֹלָם כֻּלּוֹ בְּטוּבוֹ, בְּחֵן בְּחֶסֶד וּבְרַחֲמִים. הוּא נוֹתֵן לֶחֶם לְכָל בָּשָׂר כִּי לְעוֹלָם חַסְדּוֹ. וּבְטוּבוֹ הַגָּדוֹל תָּמִיד לֹא חָסַר לָנוּ וְאַל יֶחְסַר לָנוּ מָזוֹן לְעוֹלָם וָעֶד, בַּעֲבוּר שְׁמוֹ הַגָּדוֹל, כִּי הוּא זָן וּמְפַרְנֵס לַכֹּל, וּמֵטִיב לַכֹּל וּמֵכִין מָזוֹן לְכָל בְּרִיּוֹתָיו אֲשֶׁר בָּרָא. בָּרוּךְ אַתָּה יהוה, הַזָּן אֶת הַכֹּל.

נוֹדֶה לְךָ יהוה אֱלֹהֵינוּ עַל שֶׁהִנְחַלְתָּ לַאֲבוֹתֵינוּ אֶרֶץ חֶמְדָּה טוֹבָה וּרְחָבָה, וְעַל שֶׁהוֹצֵאתָנוּ יהוה אֱלֹהֵינוּ מֵאֶרֶץ מִצְרַיִם, וּפְדִיתָנוּ מִבֵּית עֲבָדִים, וְעַל בְּרִיתְךָ שֶׁחָתַמְתָּ בִּבְשָׂרֵנוּ, וְעַל תּוֹרָתְךָ שֶׁלִּמַּדְתָּנוּ, וְעַל חֻקֶּיךָ שֶׁהוֹדַעְתָּנוּ, וְעַל חַיִּים חֵן וָחֶסֶד שֶׁחוֹנַנְתָּנוּ, וְעַל אֲכִילַת מָזוֹן שָׁאַתָּה זָן וּמְפַרְנֵס אוֹתָנוּ תָּמִיד, בְּכָל יוֹם וּבְכָל עֵת וּבְכָל שָׁעָה.

וְעַל הַכֹּל יהוה אֱלֹהֵינוּ אֲנַחְנוּ מוֹדִים לָךְ וּמְבָרְכִים אוֹתָךְ. יִתְבָּרַךְ שִׁמְךָ בְּפִי כָל חַי תָּמִיד לְעוֹלָם וָעֶד, כַּכָּתוּב: וְאָכַלְתָּ וְשָׂבָעְתָּ וּבֵרַכְתָּ אֶת יהוה אֱלֹהֶיךָ עַל הָאָרֶץ הַטּוֹבָה אֲשֶׁר נָתַן לָךְ. בָּרוּךְ אַתָּה יהוה, עַל הָאָרֶץ וְעַל הַמָּזוֹן.

Praised are You. Great antiquity is ascribed to the first four benedictions. The first three blessings ("who sustains all life," "for the land and for sustenance" and "who rebuilds Jerusalem") are of biblical origin. The fourth benediction ("who is good to all") was added in the second century of the common era. We echo, in *Birkat Hamazon*, the words of Abraham, Moses, Joshua, David, Solomon and the sages of Yavneh.

He sustains the whole world. He nurtures the righteous and the wrongdoers, the faithful and the faithless, even idolaters. He provides provender for all His creatures, from the mammoth to the minuscule, those on land and those on sea, those that fly and those that creep, even the accursed serpent. And the caring Creator, concerned with all creation, demands matching concern from His children. We must feed the hungry, treat animals humanely, protect the earth of which we are custodians. Conservationists way ahead of their time, the Rabbis legislated against the profligate destruction of trees, against the despoilment of the countryside, against the pollution of the environment, against the squandering of natural resources.

Praised are You, Adonai who sustains all life. From Moses himself the Israelites are said to have learned this benediction which they began to recite in the wilderness, where their meals were truly heaven-sent.

The covenant sealed in our flesh. Why is this phrase as meaningful to women as it is to men? "All Israel is one body," declares Rabbi Isaac Luria, "and every individual Israelite is a member of that body." All of us, men and women, were present at Sinai. "Adonai our God made a covenant with us in Ḥoreb. Adonai made this covenant not just with our ancestors but with us, even us, who are all of us alive this day" (Deuteronomy 5:2–3). According to legend, Moses laid the groundwork by canvassing the wives and mothers of Israel. "Go first to the women," God advised. "If they accept, the men will follow." And so it came to pass.

We thank You for Your Torah and its precepts. Why were *we* singled out for this singular gift? And why are we so grateful for its liberating restraints? God created the Torah long before He created the world. In fact, with its help and for its sake, the world came into being. It was offered, we are told, to all the nations of the earth. Yet when they learned that acceptance would involve onerous obligations, the would-be recipients declined the honor. Only Israel chose with unique unanimity to accept, espousing it not as a burden but as a bride, even though this bride demanded total fidelity, constant devotion. For the privilege of receiving the Torah, Jews have paid an awesome price; paid with their lives, and their children's lives. Yet this alliance can never be sundered. We see the Torah as the source of our strength, and the reason for our existence. We equate it with light and with life . . . here and Hereafter. Manifest yet mysterious, revealed yet concealed, accessible yet fathomless, lucid yet labyrinthine . . . was ever a gift so loaded with cosmic consequence?

The others respond:

Praised be (our God) the One of whose bounty we have partaken and by whose goodness we live.

Barukh (eloheinu) she'akhalnu mishelo uv'tuvo ḥayinu.

The leader continues:

Praised be (our God) the One of whose bounty we have partaken and by whose goodness we live.

Barukh (eloheinu) she'akhalnu mishelo uv'tuvo ḥayinu.

All together:

Praised be He and praised be His name.

Barukh hu u-varukh sh'mo.

Praised are You, Adonai our God, King of the universe who sustains the whole world with kindness and with compassion. He provides food for every creature, for His love endures forever. His great goodness has never failed us, His great glory assures us nourishment. All life is His creation and He is good to all, providing every creature with food and sustenance. Praised are You, Adonai who sustains all life.

We thank You, Adonai our God, for the pleasing, spacious, desirable land which You gave our ancestors, and for liberating us from Egyptian bondage. We thank You for the covenant sealed in our flesh, for teaching us Your Torah and its precepts, for the gift of life so graciously granted us, for the food we have eaten, for the nourishment You provide us all our days, whatever the season, whatever the time.

For all this we thank You and praise You, Adonai our God. May You forever be praised by all living things, as it is written in the Torah: "When you have eaten and are satisfied, you shall praise Adonai your God for the good land which He has given you." Praised are You, Adonai, for the land and for sustenance.

רַחֵם יהוה אֱלֹהֵינוּ עַל יִשְׂרָאֵל עַמֶּךָ, וְעַל יְרוּשָׁלַיִם עִירֶךָ, וְעַל צִיּוֹן מִשְׁכַּן כְּבוֹדֶךָ, וְעַל מַלְכוּת בֵּית דָּוִד מְשִׁיחֶךָ, וְעַל הַבַּיִת הַגָּדוֹל וְהַקָּדוֹשׁ שֶׁנִּקְרָא שִׁמְךָ עָלָיו. אֱלֹהֵינוּ אָבִינוּ, רְעֵנוּ זוּנֵנוּ, פַּרְנְסֵנוּ וְכַלְכְּלֵנוּ וְהַרְוִיחֵנוּ, וְהַרְוַח לָנוּ יהוה אֱלֹהֵינוּ מְהֵרָה מִכָּל צָרוֹתֵינוּ. וְנָא אַל תַּצְרִיכֵנוּ יהוה אֱלֹהֵינוּ לֹא לִידֵי מַתְּנַת בָּשָׂר וָדָם וְלֹא לִידֵי הַלְוָאָתָם, כִּי אִם לְיָדְךָ הַמְּלֵאָה הַפְּתוּחָה הַקְּדוֹשָׁה וְהָרְחָבָה, שֶׁלֹּא נֵבוֹשׁ וְלֹא נִכָּלֵם לְעוֹלָם וָעֶד.

On Shabbat, add:

רְצֵה וְהַחֲלִיצֵנוּ יהוה אֱלֹהֵינוּ בְּמִצְוֹתֶיךָ, וּבְמִצְוַת יוֹם הַשְּׁבִיעִי הַשַּׁבָּת הַגָּדוֹל וְהַקָּדוֹשׁ הַזֶּה, כִּי יוֹם זֶה גָּדוֹל וְקָדוֹשׁ הוּא לְפָנֶיךָ, לִשְׁבָּת בּוֹ וְלָנוּחַ בּוֹ בְּאַהֲבָה כְּמִצְוַת רְצוֹנֶךָ. בִּרְצוֹנְךָ הָנַח לָנוּ יהוה אֱלֹהֵינוּ שֶׁלֹּא תְהֵא צָרָה וְיָגוֹן וַאֲנָחָה בְּיוֹם מְנוּחָתֵנוּ. וְהַרְאֵנוּ יהוה אֱלֹהֵינוּ בְּנֶחָמַת צִיּוֹן עִירֶךָ, וּבְבִנְיַן יְרוּשָׁלַיִם עִיר קָדְשֶׁךָ, כִּי אַתָּה הוּא בַּעַל הַיְשׁוּעוֹת וּבַעַל הַנֶּחָמוֹת.

אֱלֹהֵינוּ וֵאלֹהֵי אֲבוֹתֵינוּ, יַעֲלֶה וְיָבֹא וְיַגִּיעַ וְיֵרָאֶה, וְיֵרָצֶה וְיִשָּׁמַע, וְיִפָּקֵד וְיִזָּכֵר זִכְרוֹנֵנוּ וּפִקְדוֹנֵנוּ, וְזִכְרוֹן אֲבוֹתֵינוּ, וְזִכְרוֹן מָשִׁיחַ בֶּן דָּוִד עַבְדֶּךָ, וְזִכְרוֹן יְרוּשָׁלַיִם עִיר קָדְשֶׁךָ, וְזִכְרוֹן כָּל עַמְּךָ בֵּית יִשְׂרָאֵל לְפָנֶיךָ, לִפְלֵיטָה וּלְטוֹבָה, לְחֵן וּלְחֶסֶד וּלְרַחֲמִים, וּלְחַיִּים וּלְשָׁלוֹם בְּיוֹם חַג הַמַּצּוֹת הַזֶּה. זָכְרֵנוּ יהוה אֱלֹהֵינוּ בּוֹ לְטוֹבָה, וּפָקְדֵנוּ בוֹ לִבְרָכָה, וְהוֹשִׁיעֵנוּ בוֹ לְחַיִּים. וּבִדְבַר יְשׁוּעָה וְרַחֲמִים חוּס וְחָנֵּנוּ, וְרַחֵם עָלֵינוּ, וְהוֹשִׁיעֵנוּ כִּי אֵלֶיךָ עֵינֵינוּ, כִּי אֵל חַנּוּן וְרַחוּם אָתָּה.

וּבְנֵה יְרוּשָׁלַיִם עִיר הַקֹּדֶשׁ בִּמְהֵרָה בְיָמֵינוּ. בָּרוּךְ אַתָּה יהוה, בּוֹנֵה בְרַחֲמָיו יְרוּשָׁלָיִם. אָמֵן.

The great and holy House. "Will God in very truth dwell on earth?" declaimed Solomon when he consecrated the Sanctuary in all its golden gleaming splendor. "Behold, heaven and the heaven of heavens cannot contain You; how much less this House that I have built" (I Kings 8:27). The Temple was a supreme symbol of God's presence among His children. But when it was destroyed, our hopes were not destroyed with it. For the Rabbis, like the prophets before them, insist that "the heart is God's Temple," that repentance and good deeds are the most acceptable of offerings.

May we never find ourselves in need. Unhappily, we have often found ourselves in need, desperate need. Locked out of guilds, locked into ghettoes, debarred from owning land, subject to the vagaries of repressive regimes, subject to legalized job discrimination in every field, Jews through the ages have surfeited on the *maror* of poverty. At the same time, the Jewish community has pioneered enlightened anti-poverty programs. To help the poor (and that includes the non-Jewish poor)—with food, gifts, loans, means of rehabilitation and above all, kindness—is a religious obligation of the highest order, equivalent to all the other *mitzvot* combined.

Your helping hand. Picture the scene at the Sea of Reeds. While the Israelites hesitated and Moses prayed for help, Naḥshon ben Amminadab, prince of the tribe of Judah, took the plunge and leaped into the raging waters. Others followed his example, Moses raised his rod — and only then did the great waves obediently subside. In Judaism, passivity is dispraised. God helps those who help themselves.

Gifts from flesh and blood. Freedom is diminished by dependency. The highest form of charity is to render the recipient self-sufficient, freed from the need to beg for human handouts.

Our God and God of our ancestors. Some of us take God on trust. We believe because our ancestors believed, in the light of incandescent tradition. For others, faith is rooted in reason. Both these approaches can be faulted. For to rely on instinct alone is anti-intellectual, a negation of the mental faculties God gave us. And logic without love can be sterile. But when trust and tradition are reinforced by learning, then our faith is fortified, and then we can speak with authenticity of "our God *and* the God of our ancestors."

This day of Pesah. The feast of the Passover (*hag haPesah*). The feast of unleavened bread (*hag hamatzot*). The season of our freedom (*z'man herutenu*). So what's in a name? Why does the Torah (with one exception) call this yom tov *hag hamatzot*, and why do we call it *hag haPesah*, or simply Pesah? A homiletical interpretation relates the former to the physical exodus and the latter to the spiritual exodus. Rabbi Levi Yitzhak of Berditchev, however, sees these two appellations as code words, as it were, in the loving dialogue between Israel and its Redeemer. *Hag hamatzot* calls attention to the trustfulness with which an enslaved people, unprepared and unprovisioned, followed their God into the Great Unknown. Pesah calls attention to the compassion with which God passed over the shortcomings of our forebears in order to hasten their release from bondage. *Z'man herutenu*, a term which occurs in our liturgy, celebrates our liberation as a nation, free to serve God.

Adonai our God, have mercy on Israel Your people, on Jerusalem Your city, on Zion the home of Your glory, on the kingdom of the House of David Your anointed, and on the great and holy House which is called by Your name. Our God, our Father, shelter us and shield us, sustain us, maintain us; grant us relief from all our troubles. May we never find ourselves in need of gifts or loans from flesh and blood, but may we always rely only upon Your helping hand, which is open and generous; thus we shall never suffer shame or humiliation.

On Shabbat, add:

Strengthen us, Adonai our God, with Your commandments, especially the commandment of this great and holy seventh day, that we may rest thereon, lovingly, according to Your will. May it be Your will, Adonai our God, to grant that our Shabbat rest be free of anguish, sorrow and sighing. May we behold Zion Your city consoled, Adonai our God, and Jerusalem Your holy city rebuilt. For You are Master of deliverance, Master of consolation.

Our God and God of our ancestors, on this day of Pesah remember our ancestors and be gracious to us. Consider the people standing before You praying for the days of the Messiah and for Jerusalem Your holy city. Grant us life, well-being, lovingkindness and peace. Bless us, Adonai our God, with all that is good. Remember Your promise of mercy and redemption. Be merciful to us and save us, for we place our hope in You, gracious and merciful God.

Rebuild Jerusalem the holy city, soon, in our time. Praised are You, Adonai who in His mercy rebuilds Jerusalem. Amen.

בָּרוּךְ אַתָּה יהוה אֱלֹהֵינוּ מֶלֶךְ הָעוֹלָם, הָאֵל אָבִינוּ מַלְכֵּנוּ אַדִּירֵנוּ בּוֹרְאֵנוּ גּוֹאֲלֵנוּ יוֹצְרֵנוּ קְדוֹשֵׁנוּ קְדוֹשׁ יַעֲקֹב, רוֹעֵנוּ רוֹעֵה יִשְׂרָאֵל, הַמֶּלֶךְ הַטּוֹב וְהַמֵּטִיב לַכֹּל, שֶׁבְּכָל יוֹם וָיוֹם הוּא הֵטִיב, הוּא מֵטִיב, הוּא יֵיטִיב לָנוּ. הוּא גְמָלָנוּ הוּא גוֹמְלֵנוּ הוּא יִגְמְלֵנוּ לָעַד, לְחֵן לְחֶסֶד וּלְרַחֲמִים וּלְרֶוַח, הַצָּלָה וְהַצְלָחָה, בְּרָכָה וִישׁוּעָה, נֶחָמָה פַּרְנָסָה וְכַלְכָּלָה, וְרַחֲמִים וְחַיִּים וְשָׁלוֹם וְכָל טוֹב, וּמִכָּל טוּב אַל יְחַסְּרֵנוּ.

הָרַחֲמָן, הוּא יִמְלֹךְ עָלֵינוּ לְעוֹלָם וָעֶד.

הָרַחֲמָן, הוּא יִתְבָּרַךְ בַּשָּׁמַיִם וּבָאָרֶץ.

הָרַחֲמָן, הוּא יִשְׁתַּבַּח לְדוֹר דּוֹרִים, וְיִתְפָּאַר בָּנוּ לָעַד וּלְנֵצַח נְצָחִים, וְיִתְהַדַּר בָּנוּ לָעַד וּלְעוֹלְמֵי עוֹלָמִים.

הָרַחֲמָן, הוּא יְפַרְנְסֵנוּ בְּכָבוֹד.

הָרַחֲמָן, הוּא יִשְׁבֹּר עֻלֵּנוּ מֵעַל צַוָּארֵנוּ, וְהוּא יוֹלִיכֵנוּ קוֹמְמִיּוּת לְאַרְצֵנוּ.

הָרַחֲמָן, הוּא יִשְׁלַח בְּרָכָה מְרֻבָּה בַּבַּיִת הַזֶּה, וְעַל שֻׁלְחָן זֶה שֶׁאָכַלְנוּ עָלָיו.

הָרַחֲמָן, הוּא יִשְׁלַח לָנוּ אֶת אֵלִיָּהוּ הַנָּבִיא, זָכוּר לַטּוֹב, וִיבַשֶּׂר לָנוּ בְּשׂוֹרוֹת טוֹבוֹת, יְשׁוּעוֹת וְנֶחָמוֹת.

הָרַחֲמָן, הוּא יְבָרֵךְ אֶת הָאָרֶץ הַזֹּאת וְיָגֵן עָלֶיהָ.

הָרַחֲמָן, הוּא יְבָרֵךְ אֶת מְדִינַת יִשְׂרָאֵל, רֵאשִׁית צְמִיחַת גְּאֻלָּתֵנוּ.

Father, *Redeemer*. God is incorporeal ("He exists without possessing the attribute of existence, He lives without possessing the attribute of life"), yet He is not an abstraction. "I believe," declares Yehudah Halevi's Rabbi to the King of the Khazars, "in the God of Abraham, Isaac and Jacob, who led the Israelites out of Mitzrayim with signs and miracles." Our allegiance, in other words, is not to the God of the philosophers. We believe in the God who acts in and through history, the God who redeemed our ancestors . . . and us.

The yoke of exile (galut). Since our exile began with the loss of our homeland, does not the restoration of that homeland effectively end the exile? "In a profound theological sense, Israel itself, now isolated among the nations of the world, is in *galut*. The reason inheres in its role as the people of God. Israel is the prototype of all mankind, which is in *galut*, alienated from God and exiled from the new Jerusalem, which is yet to be rebuilt." Many lovers of Zion see the reestablishment of the Jewish State as the genesis of our exodus from exile.

The prophet Elijah. How can there be amity between nation and nation, when neighbors are at odds, when households are divided? Early in the Seder the "wicked" child poses disruptive questions. The evening draws to its close with Elijah bringing harmony, *shalom bayit*, into the home, generating empathy between alienated generations, so that peace may spread in concentric circles until it envelops the whole human family.

Bless this land, bless the State of Israel. We wear coats of many colors. Many loves and many loyalties are spun into the fabric of our lives. We are patriotic citizens of the lands of the dispersion, and we order our days according to the lunar calendar. We pray for the peace of Jerusalem, and we work for the betterment of our neighborhood and our nation. Said Philo, domiciled in Alexandria, Egypt, some nineteen hundred years ago, "We who live throughout the world all owe a debt of loyalty to our fatherland. But we also have a motherland which is the holy city of Jerusalem."

The dawn of our redemption. This dawn broke with a blood-red sky. As we pray for the protection and the security of the vulnerable Jewish State, we mourn the heavy toll that this redemption took in young and gallant lives. "Seven thousand killed in 1948 in the War of Independence; another thousand killed in the 1956 Sinai Campaign and the 1967 Six-Day War; three thousand killed in the October 1973 War; hundreds killed by terrorist raids. We offer ourselves grim consolation; all the wars have cost us less than three days at Auschwitz."

Praised are You, Adonai our God, King of the universe, our Father, our King, our Creator and Redeemer who fashioned us, our Holy One and the Holy One of Jacob, our Shepherd and Shepherd of the people Israel, the King who is good to all, whose goodness is constant throughout all time. Bestow upon us grace, kindness and compassion, providing us deliverance, prosperity and ease, life and peace and all goodness. May we never be denied the good things of life.

May the Merciful reign over us throughout all time.

May the Merciful be praised in heaven and on earth.

May the Merciful be lauded in every generation, glorified through our lives, exalted through us always and for all eternity.

May the Merciful enable us to earn our livelihood honorably.

May the Merciful lift the yoke of exile and lead us in dignity to our land.

May the Merciful send a full measure of blessing to this house and to this table at which we have eaten.

May the Merciful send us the prophet Elijah, whose good deeds we remember, who will bring us good tidings of deliverance and comfort.

May the Merciful bless this land and protect it.

May the Merciful bless the State of Israel, the dawn of our redemption.

הָרַחֲמָן, הוּא יְבָרֵךְ אֶת אַחֵינוּ בְּנֵי יִשְׂרָאֵל הַנְּתוּנִים בְּצָרָה, וְיוֹצִיאֵם מֵאֲפֵלָה לְאוֹרָה.

הָרַחֲמָן, הוּא יְבָרֵךְ אֶת (אָבִי מוֹרִי) בַּעַל הַבַּיִת הַזֶּה, וְאֶת (אִמִּי מוֹרָתִי) בַּעֲלַת הַבַּיִת הַזֶּה, אוֹתָם וְאֶת בֵּיתָם (וְאֶת זַרְעָם) וְאֶת כָּל אֲשֶׁר לָהֶם, אוֹתָנוּ וְאֶת כָּל אֲשֶׁר לָנוּ, (וְאֶת כָּל הַמְּסֻבִּים כַּאן) כְּמוֹ שֶׁנִּתְבָּרְכוּ אֲבוֹתֵינוּ אַבְרָהָם יִצְחָק וְיַעֲקֹב בַּכֹּל מִכֹּל כֹּל. כֵּן יְבָרֵךְ אוֹתָנוּ כֻּלָּנוּ יַחַד בִּבְרָכָה שְׁלֵמָה, וְנֹאמַר אָמֵן.

בַּמָּרוֹם יְלַמְּדוּ עֲלֵיהֶם וְעָלֵינוּ זְכוּת שֶׁתְּהִי לְמִשְׁמֶרֶת שָׁלוֹם. וְנִשָּׂא בְרָכָה מֵאֵת יהוה וּצְדָקָה מֵאֱלֹהֵי יִשְׁעֵנוּ, וְנִמְצָא חֵן וְשֵׂכֶל טוֹב בְּעֵינֵי אֱלֹהִים וְאָדָם.

On Shabbat, add:

הָרַחֲמָן, הוּא יַנְחִילֵנוּ יוֹם שֶׁכֻּלּוֹ שַׁבָּת וּמְנוּחָה לְחַיֵּי הָעוֹלָמִים.

הָרַחֲמָן, הוּא יַנְחִילֵנוּ יוֹם שֶׁכֻּלּוֹ טוֹב, שֶׁצַּדִּיקִים יוֹשְׁבִים וְעַטְרוֹתֵיהֶם בְּרָאשֵׁיהֶם וְנֶהֱנִים מִזִּיו הַשְּׁכִינָה, וְיִהְיֶה חֶלְקֵנוּ עִמָּהֶם.

הָרַחֲמָן, הוּא יְזַכֵּנוּ לִימוֹת הַמָּשִׁיחַ וּלְחַיֵּי הָעוֹלָם הַבָּא. מִגְדּוֹל יְשׁוּעוֹת מַלְכּוֹ וְעֹשֶׂה חֶסֶד לִמְשִׁיחוֹ לְדָוִד וּלְזַרְעוֹ עַד עוֹלָם. עֹשֶׂה שָׁלוֹם בִּמְרוֹמָיו הוּא יַעֲשֶׂה שָׁלוֹם עָלֵינוּ וְעַל כָּל יִשְׂרָאֵל, וְאִמְרוּ אָמֵן.

יְראוּ אֶת יהוה קְדֹשָׁיו, כִּי אֵין מַחְסוֹר לִירֵאָיו. כְּפִירִים רָשׁוּ וְרָעֵבוּ, וְדֹרְשֵׁי יהוה לֹא יַחְסְרוּ כָל טוֹב. הוֹדוּ לַיהוה כִּי טוֹב, כִּי לְעוֹלָם חַסְדּוֹ. פּוֹתֵחַ אֶת יָדֶךָ וּמַשְׂבִּיעַ לְכָל חַי רָצוֹן. בָּרוּךְ הַגֶּבֶר אֲשֶׁר יִבְטַח בַּיהוה, וְהָיָה יהוה מִבְטַחוֹ. נַעַר הָיִיתִי גַּם זָקַנְתִּי וְלֹא רָאִיתִי צַדִּיק נֶעֱזָב וְזַרְעוֹ מְבַקֶּשׁ לָחֶם. יהוה עֹז לְעַמּוֹ יִתֵּן, יהוה יְבָרֵךְ אֶת עַמּוֹ בַשָּׁלוֹם.

My father, my mother. The Hebrew text refers to "my father, my teacher" and "my mother, my teacher." Transmitting Judaism's living legacy to coming generations is the surest way to thwart the pharaohs who have tried over and again to murder our children. "Our paramount concern is to educate our sons and daughters well." The words are the words of Josephus, but the voice is the voice of Jewish parents through the ages.

He blessed our fathers. There were many tribes who walked the same desert as the seed of Abraham. They were descended from similar stock, spoke related languages, breathed the same air, shared the same sun; but one was chosen by God to be catapulted across the horizon of history to write its flaming message indelibly upon the human heart.

Abraham, Isaac and Jacob are not principles to be comprehended but lives to be continued.

The life of eternity. A certain individual was once vouchsafed a vision of the world to come, and in this vision he saw scholars deeply immersed in the study of the Torah. "This," he exclaimed in disappointment, "is heaven?" "You think the sages are in Paradise?" a heavenly voice rebuked him. "No! Paradise is in the sages!"

Bringing peace. Heaven (*shamayim*) came into being when God made peace between fire (*esh*) and water (*mayim*). If God can create harmony between such elemental opposites, then surely we can resolve our often trifling differences and help to create peace on earth.

86

The righteous with crowns on their heads. These crowns evoke an image of the Greek games, culminating for most contestants in ignominious defeat, with laurel wreaths reserved for the victorious elite. But for the Rabbis the race is not to the swift, and there need be no losers in the game of life. All can win. For all can aspire to and attain the most precious of prizes: the crown of learning.

The righteous sit with crowns on their heads. The Torah is noticeably reticent on the subject of the Hereafter. While the Rabbis assure us that this world is but the passageway leading to the world of eternity, they urge us to concentrate on living a full life here and now, a life full of Torah and good deeds. And when we make the transition from the finite to the infinite, what then? This is how one Talmudist portrays Paradise: "There is neither eating nor drinking nor procreation nor preoccupation with business, neither jealousy nor hatred nor rivalry, but the righteous sit with crowns on their heads, enjoying the splendor of the Divine Presence."

I have not seen the righteous forsaken. We *are* our brother's keeper. However, we are not our brother's judge. Whether he is "righteous" or not, we cannot look on, apathetic and indifferent, when we see him impoverished or in distress. Moses, brought up in Pharaoh's palace, could have settled for a life of princely privilege. Instead, he went out to help his people, toiling alongside them, intervening on their behalf, trying to lighten their burdens and their spirits. "Every man for himself" is not a Jewish credo.

May the Merciful bless those of our people who are in trouble and bring them out of darkness into light.

May the Merciful bless (my father) our host and (my mother) our hostess, together with their children and all that is theirs (me and my family and all that is mine). May He bless us and all that is ours (and may He bless all who are gathered here), as He blessed our fathers, Abraham, Isaac and Jacob, in everything. May He fully bless each and all of us. And let us say: Amen.

May our merit be invoked on high, leading to enduring peace. May we receive blessings from Adonai, lovingkindness from the God of our deliverance. May we be found pleasing in the sight of both God and mortals.

On Shabbat, add:
May the Merciful grant us a day of Shabbat rest, a foretaste of the world to come.

May the Merciful grant us a share in eternity, in the company of the righteous who sit with crowns on their heads, enjoying the splendor of the *Sh'khinah*.

May the Merciful consider us worthy of the messianic era and life in the world to come. He bestows salvation and lovingkindness upon His king, upon His anointed, upon David and his descendants forevermore. May He who brings peace to His universe bring peace to us, and to all Israel. And let us say: Amen.

May His holy ones revere him, for those who revere Adonai know no want. Scoffers may suffer want and hunger, but those who seek Adonai shall lack nothing. Give thanks to Adonai, for He is good; His love endures forever. He opens His hand and satisfies every living thing with favor. Blessed are those who trust in Adonai, whose trust is Adonai. "I have been young and now I am old," says the Psalmist, "yet I have not seen the righteous forsaken, nor their children begging for bread." May Adonai grant His people strength. May Adonai bless His people with peace.

ברכת המזון

On Shabbat and festivals, Psalm 126, shir hama'alot (page 78) is recited before Birkat Hamazon.

When three or more adults have eaten together, one of them formally invites the others to join in these blessings. (When ten or more are present, the words in parentheses are added.)

The leader:

רַבּוֹתַי נְבָרֵךְ.

The others respond:

יְהִי שֵׁם יהוה מְבֹרָךְ מֵעַתָּה וְעַד עוֹלָם.

The leader continues:

יְהִי שֵׁם יהוה מְבֹרָךְ מֵעַתָּה וְעַד עוֹלָם.
בִּרְשׁוּת רַבּוֹתַי, נְבָרֵךְ (אֱלֹהֵינוּ) שֶׁאָכַלְנוּ מִשֶּׁלּוֹ.

The others respond:

בָּרוּךְ (אֱלֹהֵינוּ) שֶׁאָכַלְנוּ מִשֶּׁלּוֹ וּבְטוּבוֹ חָיִינוּ.

The leader continues:

בָּרוּךְ (אֱלֹהֵינוּ) שֶׁאָכַלְנוּ מִשֶּׁלּוֹ וּבְטוּבוֹ חָיִינוּ.

All together:

בָּרוּךְ הוּא וּבָרוּךְ שְׁמוֹ.

Blessings After the Meal
Short Version

On Shabbat and festivals, Psalm 126, shir hama'alot (page 79) is recited before Birkat Hamazon.

Short version. This is an expanded version of the *Birkat Hamazon* that appears in one of the oldest existing Jewish prayerbooks, the *siddur* of 10th century Saadia Gaon. The Rabbis believe that there is a time for prolonged devotions and a time for brevity. We are told that when the Israelites arrived at the Red Sea and Moses sought divine guidance in protracted supplications, he evoked a terse rejoinder from on high: "My children are in danger, the sea in front of them and the enemy behind them, and you stand there, praying!" It should be noted, though, that Moses had occasion to utter one of the briefest prayers on record. When his sister was stricken, he pleaded for her, in five Hebrew words: "God, please heal her now!" (*Eil na refa na la*) (Numbers 12:13). And Miriam was healed.

When three or more adults have eaten together, one of them formally invites the others to join in these blessings. (When ten or more are present, the words in parentheses are added.)

The leader:

Friends, let us give thanks.

Rabotai n'varekh.

The others respond:

May Adonai be praised, now and forever.

Yehi shem adonai m'vorakh mei-attah v'ad olam.

The leader continues:

May Adonai be praised, now and forever.
With your consent, friends, let us praise (our God) the One whose food we have eaten.

Yehi shem adonai m'vorakh mei-attah v'ad olam.
Bir'shut rabotai, n'varekh (eloheinu) she-akhalnu mishelo.

The others respond:

Praised be (our God) the One of whose bounty we have partaken and by whose goodness we live.

Barukh (eloheinu) she'akhalnu mishelo uv'tuvo ḥayinu.

The leader continues:

Praised be (our God) the One of whose bounty we have partaken and by whose goodness we live.

Barukh (eloheinu) she'akhalnu mishelo uv'tuvo ḥayinu.

All together:

Praised be He and praised be His name.

Barukh hu u'varukh sh'mo.

בָּרוּךְ אַתָּה יהוה אֱלֹהֵינוּ מֶלֶךְ הָעוֹלָם, הַזָּן אֶת הָעוֹלָם כֻּלּוֹ בְּטוּבוֹ, בְּחֵן בְּחֶסֶד וּבְרַחֲמִים. הוּא נוֹתֵן לֶחֶם לְכָל בָּשָׂר כִּי לְעוֹלָם חַסְדּוֹ. וּבְטוּבוֹ הַגָּדוֹל תָּמִיד לֹא חָסַר לָנוּ וְאַל יֶחְסַר לָנוּ מָזוֹן לְעוֹלָם וָעֶד, בַּעֲבוּר שְׁמוֹ הַגָּדוֹל, כִּי הוּא זָן וּמְפַרְנֵס לַכֹּל, וּמֵטִיב לַכֹּל וּמֵכִין מָזוֹן לְכָל בְּרִיּוֹתָיו אֲשֶׁר בָּרָא. בָּרוּךְ אַתָּה יהוה, הַזָּן אֶת הַכֹּל.

נוֹדֶה לְךָ יהוה אֱלֹהֵינוּ עַל שֶׁהִנְחַלְתָּ לַאֲבוֹתֵינוּ אֶרֶץ חֶמְדָּה טוֹבָה וּרְחָבָה, בְּרִית וְתוֹרָה, חַיִּים וּמָזוֹן. יִתְבָּרַךְ שִׁמְךָ בְּפִי כָל חַי תָּמִיד לְעוֹלָם וָעֶד, כַּכָּתוּב: וְאָכַלְתָּ וְשָׂבָעְתָּ וּבֵרַכְתָּ אֶת יהוה אֱלֹהֶיךָ עַל הָאָרֶץ הַטּוֹבָה אֲשֶׁר נָתַן לָךְ. בָּרוּךְ אַתָּה יהוה, עַל הָאָרֶץ וְעַל הַמָּזוֹן.

On Shabbat, add:

רְצֵה וְהַחֲלִיצֵנוּ יהוה אֱלֹהֵינוּ בְּמִצְוֹתֶיךָ, וּבְמִצְוַת יוֹם הַשְּׁבִיעִי הַשַּׁבָּת הַגָּדוֹל וְהַקָּדוֹשׁ הַזֶּה, כִּי יוֹם זֶה גָּדוֹל וְקָדוֹשׁ הוּא לְפָנֶיךָ, לִשְׁבָּת בּוֹ וְלָנוּחַ בּוֹ בְּאַהֲבָה כְּמִצְוַת רְצוֹנֶךָ. בִּרְצוֹנְךָ הָנַח לָנוּ יהוה אֱלֹהֵינוּ שֶׁלֹּא תְהִי צָרָה וְיָגוֹן וַאֲנָחָה בְּיוֹם מְנוּחָתֵנוּ.

אֱלֹהֵינוּ וֵאלֹהֵי אֲבוֹתֵינוּ, יַעֲלֶה וְיָבוֹא, יַגִּיעַ וְיֵרָאֶה, יֵרָצֶה וְיִפָּקֵד זִכְרוֹנֵנוּ וְזִכְרוֹן אֲבוֹתֵינוּ, וְזִכְרוֹן יְרוּשָׁלַיִם עִירֶךָ, וְזִכְרוֹן עַמְּךָ כָּל בֵּית יִשְׂרָאֵל לְפָנֶיךָ לְטוֹבָה בְּיוֹם חַג הַמַּצּוֹת הַזֶּה. זָכְרֵנוּ יהוה אֱלֹהֵינוּ בּוֹ לְטוֹבָה, וּפָקְדֵנוּ בּוֹ לִבְרָכָה, וְהוֹשִׁיעֵנוּ בּוֹ לְחַיִּים.

רַחֵם יהוה אֱלֹהֵינוּ עַל יִשְׂרָאֵל עַמֶּךָ וְעַל מַלְכוּת בֵּית דָּוִד מְשִׁיחֶךָ. וּבְנֵה יְרוּשָׁלַיִם עִיר הַקֹּדֶשׁ בִּמְהֵרָה בְיָמֵינוּ. בָּרוּךְ אַתָּה יהוה, בּוֹנֶה בְרַחֲמָיו יְרוּשָׁלָיִם. אָמֵן.

For all this we thank You. We are not required to renounce the good things in life (on the contrary, we are encouraged to enjoy "permissible pleasures"), but we *are* required to remember the source of all goodness. "All things in the world and the world itself are a free gift, an act of grace and kindness on God's part." *Birkat Hamazon* was instituted by the Rabbis on the basis of this verse: "When you have eaten and are satisfied, you shall praise Adonai" (Deuteronomy 8:10).

We thank You . . . for the land. Generals do not generally compose benedictions. But the Rabbis tell us that Joshua, a most atypical commander, poised at the threshold of the Holy Land, about to reclaim Israel's rightful God-given patrimony, was moved to utter these blessings. The thought of *Eretz Yisrael*, deeded to us by the greatest Landlord of them all, is hardly buried in our national subconscious. Nor do we take this most gracious grant for granted. We speak of it every day, at every meal, prayerfully.

Shabbat rest. Although it was not until Sinai that the union between Israel and Shabbat was officially consummated, it is said that it was at the instigation of Moses that the Israelites began to observe Shabbat in Mitzrayim. Appealing to Pharaoh's self-interest, Moses spoke in terms of increased productivity, claiming that the serfs would work harder if they were granted a weekly respite. Pharaoh acquiesced, Moses appointed Shabbat the day of rest, and it became a day of refuge and renewal, restoring body and soul. How could Pharaoh know that he was virtually underwriting our survival as Jews? How could Pharaoh know that the arrangement would blossom into a permanent love affair, a *rapprochement* of remarkable reciprocity? "More than Israel has kept Shabbat," comments Aḥad HaAm, "Shabbat has kept Israel."

Holy city, holy land. Holiness was innate in *Eretz Yisrael* from time immemorial, save that none knew of it until our father Abraham came and began to reveal the holiness of the land. For he was a man of love. Love that seeks no return was the quality with which he sustained the world before the Torah was given, and it was this very love that was hidden in *Eretz Yisrael.* It was the hidden Torah, for the Land of Israel and the Torah are one and the same thing. Then, when the Israelites received the Torah and came to *Eretz Yisrael*, they were able to lift hidden holiness into the open.

Praised are You, Adonai our God, King of the universe who sustains the whole world with kindness and compassion. He provides food for every creature, for His love endures forever. His great goodness has never failed us. His great glory assures us nourishment. All life is His creation and He is good to all, providing every creature with food and sustenance. Praised are You, Adonai who sustains all life.

We thank You, Adonai our God, for the pleasing, spacious, desirable land which You gave our ancestors, for the covenant and the Torah, for life and sustenance. May You forever be praised by all living things, as it is written in the Torah, "When you have eaten and are satisfied, you shall praise Adonai your God for the good land which He has given you." Praised are You, Adonai, for the land and for sustenance.

On Shabbat, add:

Strengthen us, Adonai our God, with Your commandments, especially the commandment of this great and holy seventh day, that we may rest thereon, lovingly, according to Your will. May it be Your will, Adonai our God, to grant that our Shabbat rest be free of anguish, sorrow and sighing.

Our God and God of our ancestors, on this Pesaḥ remember our ancestors and be gracious to us. Consider Your people Israel standing before You today, praying for Jerusalem Your city. Bless us, Adonai our God, with all that is good. Remember us this day for blessing, rescue us with life.

Show mercy, Adonai our God, towards Your people Israel, and toward the royal House of David Your Messiah. Rebuild Jerusalem, Your holy city, soon, in our time. Praised are You, Adonai who in His mercy rebuilds Jerusalem. Amen.

בָּרוּךְ אַתָּה יהוה אֱלֹהֵינוּ מֶלֶךְ הָעוֹלָם, הַמֶּלֶךְ הַטּוֹב וְהַמֵּטִיב לַכֹּל. הוּא הֵטִיב, הוּא מֵטִיב, הוּא יֵיטִיב לָנוּ. הוּא גְמָלָנוּ הוּא גוֹמְלֵנוּ הוּא יִגְמְלֵנוּ לָעַד, חֵן חֶסֶד וְרַחֲמִים, וִיזַכֵּנוּ לִימוֹת הַמָּשִׁיחַ.

הָרַחֲמָן, הוּא יְבָרֵךְ אֶת כָּל הַמְסֻבִּים כַּאן.

On Shabbat, add:

הָרַחֲמָן, הוּא יַנְחִילֵנוּ יוֹם שֶׁכֻּלּוֹ שַׁבָּת וּמְנוּחָה לְחַיֵּי הָעוֹלָמִים.

הָרַחֲמָן, הוּא יַנְחִילֵנוּ יוֹם שֶׁכֻּלּוֹ טוֹב.

מַה שֶּׁאָכַלְנוּ יִהְיֶה לְשָׂבְעָה
וּמַה שֶּׁשָּׁתִינוּ יִהְיֶה לִרְפוּאָה.
וּמַה שֶּׁהוֹתַרְנוּ יִהְיֶה לִבְרָכָה, כְּדִכְתִיב
וַיִּתֵּן לִפְנֵיהֶם וַיֹּאכְלוּ וַיּוֹתִירוּ כִּדְבַר יהוה.

יהוה עֹז לְעַמּוֹ יִתֵּן, יהוה יְבָרֵךְ אֶת עַמּוֹ בַשָּׁלוֹם.

כוס שלישי

Reflection:

הִנְנִי מוּכָן/מוּכָנָה וּמְזֻמָּן/וּמְזֻמֶּנֶת לְקַיֵּם מִצְוַת כּוֹס שְׁלִישִׁי שֶׁהוּא כְּנֶגֶד בְּשׂוֹרַת הַיְשׁוּעָה שֶׁאָמַר הַקָּדוֹשׁ בָּרוּךְ הוּא לְיִשְׂרָאֵל: וְגָאַלְתִּי אֶתְכֶם בִּזְרוֹעַ נְטוּיָה וּבִשְׁפָטִים גְּדוֹלִים.

Lift the cup of wine and recite:

בָּרוּךְ אַתָּה יהוה אֱלֹהֵינוּ מֶלֶךְ הָעוֹלָם בּוֹרֵא פְּרִי הַגָּפֶן.

Drink the wine while reclining.

The days of the Messiah. But how long will he tarry? For millennia we have expected him momentarily. For millennia we have listened for his footsteps. For millennia we have lived in hope. Through fasting, through meditation, through prayer, through esoteric computations, the faithful have endeavored to accelerate his advent, or at least to arrive at the divinely scheduled date of his arrival. But this remains the best-kept secret of the ages. Like shooting stars, pseudo-redeemers rose and fell, leaving tragedy in their wake. Yet still the messianic hope blazed like a beacon through the gloom and doom of the exile. The seers said that the Messiah would come when humanity was "all good or all bad." They said he would come when we had given up hope that he would ever come. They said he would come when Israel observed even one Shabbat wholeheartedly. They said he would come when he came. And when he comes, then what? "No hunger. No warfare. No jealousy. No strife. Prosperity everywhere. Blessings in superabundance. And the world will be wholly occupied with acquiring knowledge of God."

Some believe that redemption—like revelation—is continuous and that every human being is intimately implicated in the process, endowed with the ability to help or hinder, advance or delay it. They see in every soul, in every action, a redemptive spark. So every one of us counts and everything we do matters. Together we can perfect ourselves, and complete creation. Together we can help to restore cosmic harmony. And bring about the beginning of the End of Days.

It is told of Elisha. This allusion to the prophet and wonderworker Elisha, heir to the mantle of Elijah, appears in the Sephardic *Birkat Hamazon.*

May He bring peace. Etymologically, peace (*shalom*) comes from a root meaning to perfect, to complete, for without peace our life, our world, is indeed imperfect and incomplete. Consequently, it is not enough to pray for peace. While we observe most commandments when and as the opportunities present themselves, we must go out of our way to "seek peace and pursue it" (Psalms 34:15).

Praised are You, Adonai our God, King of the universe who is good to all, whose goodness is constant throughout all time. Favor us with kindness and compassion now and in the future as in the past. May we be worthy of the days of the Messiah.

May the Merciful bless all who are gathered here.

On Shabbat, add:

May the Merciful grant us a day of Shabbat rest, a foretaste of the world to come.

May the Merciful grant us a day of unspoiled goodness.

May we be satisfied with what we have eaten. May we be content with what we have drunk. May what remains benefit others, even as it is told of Elisha that he set twenty loaves of barley before throngs of people, and they ate and food was left over, according to the word of Adonai (II Kings 4:42–44).

May Adonai grant His people strength.
May Adonai bless His people with peace.

The Third Cup

Reflection:

I am ready to fulfill the commandment of drinking the third of the Four Cups. This recalls God's promise of redemption to the people Israel, as it says, "I will redeem you with an outstretched arm and through extraordinary judgments" (Exodus 6:6).

Lift the cup of wine and recite:

Praised are You, Adonai our God, King of the universe who creates the fruit of the vine.

Drink the wine while reclining.

In Every Generation

From this mini-anthology of writings ancient and recent, you may wish to select readings to include in your Seder celebration. The objective? To enrich and intensify your own Exodus experience, so that, in the words of Rav Kook, "the old may become new and the new may become holy." We have retraced our passage from slavery to freedom, from Mitzrayim to Mount Sinai. Now we take up the tale again, for new chapters continue to unfold. For two thousand years we wander through desert and dale — multitudes, multitudes, in the valley of derision — welcome, unwelcome, tolerated, taunted, harbored, haunted . . . as we journey towards the Promised Land.

Erev Pesaḥ 1943. The Battle of the Warsaw Ghetto started on the first night of Pesaḥ. For twenty-eight shattering days, while the world watched in silence, a handful of men, women and children pitted their fragility against the massed might of the Nazi war machine. Although the flames have long been extinguished, the embers still smolder. For Pharaohs come and Pharaohs go: the Sennacheribs, the Belshazzars, the Hamans. But the Freedom Fighters of the Ghetto will live for ever, fiery testimony to the love of liberty kindled by the Exodus. Once more the Covenant People had kept the faith.

Master of the universe, I do not know what questions to ask. I do not expect You to reveal Your secrets to me. All I ask is that You show me one thing—what this moment means to me and what You demand of me. I do not ask why I suffer. I ask only this: Do I suffer for Your sake?

Rabbi Levi Yitzḥak of Berditchev

In the Warsaw Ghetto it's Pesaḥ once more.
The cup of Elijah is filled to the brim.
The faithful recount the deliverance of yore,
But in storms the Angel of Death, baleful, grim.
As always, the barking of germans is heard.
As always, the snarling of mad dogs of hate.
They have come here, these jackbooted pharaohs, to herd
Israel's innocent lambs to their terrible fate.
But never again will Jews tolerate taunts,
Never again obey death-bearing orders.
The doorposts tonight will be crimson with blood,
The blood of the murderers, freedom's destroyers.

Bunim Heller

אין וואַרשעוװער געטאָ איז איצט חודש ניסן,

און פול שטייט דער כּוס אליהו הנביאס,

נאָר ווער האָט דעם סדר דאָ איבערגעריסן ?

פון כּוס וועט באַלד טרינקען דער מלאך המות.

ווי שטענדיק — די דייטשישע שפּראַך פון מושטרירן,

ווי שטענדיק — די שפּראַך פון באַפעלן געניטע.

ווי שטענדיק — זיי זענען געקומען איצט פירן

אַ טייל פונעם יידישן פאָלק צו דער שחיטה.

נאָר מער וויל דאָס געטאָ נישט הערן דאָס זידלען

פון נאַציס, וואָס פירן אַ פאָלק צו פאַרלענדונג,

מיט בלוט וועט מען איצטער באַשמירן די שטידלען,

מיט בלוט פון די דייטשן, מיט בלוט פון די שענדער.

בינם העלער

The Jews in Bergen-Belsen had no matzot for Pesaḥ 1944. It was decided that it was permissible to eat ḥametz, and that the following prayer should be recited before eating:

"Our Father in Heaven, behold, it is evident and known to You that it is our desire to do Your will and to celebrate the festival of Pesaḥ by eating *matzah* and by observing the prohibition against *ḥametz*. But our hearts are pained that the enslavement prevents us from doing so, and our lives are in danger. Behold, we are ready to fulfill Your commandment, 'And you shall live by them and not die by them.' Therefore, our prayer to You is that You may keep us alive and save us and rescue us speedily so that we may observe Your commandments and do Your will and serve You with a perfect heart. Amen."

Prayer recited in Bergen-Belsen before eating ḥametz:

אָבִינוּ שֶׁבַּשָּׁמַיִם, הִנֵּה גָּלוּי וְיָדוּעַ לְפָנֶיךָ שֶׁרְצוֹנֵנוּ
לַעֲשׂוֹת רְצוֹנְךָ וְלָחוֹג אֶת חַג הַפֶּסַח בַּאֲכִילַת מַצָּה
וּבִשְׁמִירַת אִיסוּר חָמֵץ. אַף עַל זֹאת דָּאֲבָה לִבֵּנוּ
שֶׁהַשִּׁעְבּוּד מְעַכֵּב אוֹתָנוּ וַאֲנַחְנוּ נִמְצָאִים בְּסַכָּנַת
נְפָשׁוֹת. הִנְנוּ מוּכָנִים וּמְזֻמָּנִים לְקַיֵּם מִצְוָתְךָ: וְחַי
בָּהֶם וְלֹא שֶׁיָּמוּת בָּהֶם, וְלִזָּהֵר מֵאַזְהָרָה „הִזָּהֵר לְךָ
וּשְׁמוֹר נַפְשְׁךָ מְאוֹד", וְעַל כֵּן תְּפִלָּתֵנוּ לְךָ שֶׁתְּחַיֵּינוּ
וּתְקַיְּמֵנוּ וְתִגְאָלֵנוּ בִּמְהֵרָה לִשְׁמוֹר חוּקֶּיךָ וְלַעֲשׂוֹת
רְצוֹנֶךָ וּלְעָבְדְּךָ בְּלֵבָב שָׁלֵם. אָמֵן.

On this Seder night, we recall with anguish and with love
our martyred brothers and sisters, the six million Jews of Europe
who were destroyed at the hands of a tyrant more fiendish than
Pharaoh. Their memory will never be forgotten. Their murderers will never be forgiven.

Trapped in ghettoes, caged in death camps, abandoned by
an unseeing or uncaring world, Jews gave their lives in acts that
sanctified God's name and the name of His people Israel. Some
rebelled against their tormentors, fighting with makeshift
weapons, gathering the last remnants of their failing strength in
peerless gestures of courage and defiance. Others went to their
death with their faith in God miraculously unimpaired.

Unchecked, unchallenged, evil ran rampant and devoured
the holy innocents. But the light of the Six Million will never be
extinguished. Their glow illumines our path. And we will teach
our children and our children's children to remember them with
reverence and with pride.

We invite the souls of all who are missing, the souls of all
who were snatched from our midst, to sit with us together at the
Seder. This invitation was uttered by Seder celebrants in the
Vilna Ghetto in 1942 . . . and we repeat it tonight. For on this
night all Jews are united in history and in hope. We were all in
Mitzrayim. We were all at Sinai. We were all in the hell that was
the Holocaust. And we will all be present at the final redemption.

Shimon Grilius spent five years in a Soviet labor camp as a prisoner of conscience. His crime? His desire to live in Israel. When he finally immigrated in 1974, he opened a yeshiva in Jerusalem for Russian olim. This is an extract from his prison journal:

We held the Seder in a hurry, as in the time of the Exodus from Mitzrayim, since the camp authorities prohibited the holding of a Seder. Instead of *maror*, we ate slices of onion, and for *zeroa*, we used burnt soup cubes. We read from one Haggadah, the only copy we had, and when we reached *korekh*, we had nothing to put between the *matzot*. Then Iosif Mendelevich said, "We do not need a symbol of our suffering. We have real suffering and we shall put that between the *matzot*."

Anatoly Shcharansky first applied to the Soviet government for permission to emigrate to Israel in 1973. After years of escalating harassment, he was arrested for "treason" in 1977, and separated from his wife, Avital, one day after their marriage. When the Soviet court imposed its harsh sentence, he made this statement:

Five years ago, I submitted my application for exit to Israel. Now I am further than ever from my dream. It would seem to be cause for regret. But it is absolutely otherwise. I am happy. I am happy that I lived honestly, in peace with my conscience. I never compromised my soul, even under the threat of death.

I am happy that I helped people. I am proud that I knew and worked with such honest, brave and courageous people as Sakharov, Orlov, Ginsburg, who are carrying on the traditions of Russian intelligentsia. I am fortunate to have been witness to the process of the liberation of Russia's Jews.

I hope that the absurd accusation against me and the entire Jewish emigration movement will not hinder the liberation of my people. My near ones and friends know how I wanted to exchange activity in the emigration movement for a life with my wife, Avital, in Israel.

For more than 2,000 years the Jewish people, my people, have been dispersed. But wherever they are, wherever Jews are found, every year they have repeated, "Next year in Jerusalem." Now, when I am further than ever from my people, from Avital, facing many arduous years of imprisonment, I say, turning to my people, my Avital: Next year in Jerusalem.

אֲנִי מַאֲמִין בֶּאֱמוּנָה שְׁלֵמָה
בְּבִיאַת הַמָּשִׁיחַ. וְאַף עַל פִּי
שֶׁיִתְמַהְמֵהַּ, עִם כָּל זֶה
אֲחַכֶּה לוֹ בְּכָל יוֹם שֶׁיָּבֹא.

Ani ma'amin b'emunah shleimah
b'viat ha-mashiaḥ. V'af al pi
she-yit-mah-mei-ah, im kol zeh
aḥakeh lo b'khol yom sheyavo.

Ani ma'amin.
I believe with all my heart
in the coming of the Messiah,
and even though he may tarry,
I will wait each and every day
for his arrival.
Maimonides, 12th century

Ani ma'amin.
I believe in the sun
even when it is not shining.
I believe in love
even when I do not feel it.
I believe in God
even when He is silent.
Jews in Germany, 1939

100

Why does this impassioned invocation of divine wrath belong in our celebration of freedom? Because, by opting conveniently for chronic amnesia, the world compels us to remember freedom's foes.

So we remember. The Hadrianic persecutions. The Crusades. The ritual murder accusations. The Inquisition. The pogroms. The Holocaust. And we remember the God-fearing men and women of all nations who risked their lives for us in so many valleys of the shadow of death.

We are forbidden to hate the Egyptians. Yet we are enjoined to remember the crimes of the Amalekites. We are commanded to feed our enemy when he is hungry. We are warned to leave the avenging to the God of justice. Remembrance. Gratefulness. Retribution. Restraint. Should we struggle to reconcile these complicated and conflicting emotions, or should we simply accept the fact that they coexist?

Jewish existence is a tapestry woven of silk on a loom of steel, woven with tears and blood, mystery and martyrdom, threnody, exultation, anguish, ecstasy, peril and paradox. We will never forfeit that most desirable of designations, merciful children of the merciful God, raḥmanim b'nei raḥmanim. And we will never forget the Amalekites.

Fill Elijah's goblet and the Fourth Cup. The leader fills Elijah's goblet, or passes it round the table so that every participant can add some wine from his or her own cup. Rabbi Naftali of Ropschitz used to fill Elijah's goblet in this communal fashion to demonstrate that we must work together to bring about redemption. "Only through its own efforts," declare the sages, "will Israel be redeemed." We open the door for Elijah (usually a child is given this privilege) as we rise and recite:

שְׁפֹךְ חֲמָתְךָ אֶל הַגּוֹיִם אֲשֶׁר לֹא יְדָעוּךָ

וְעַל מַמְלָכוֹת אֲשֶׁר בְּשִׁמְךָ לֹא קָרָאוּ.

כִּי אָכַל אֶת יַעֲקֹב וְאֶת נָוֵהוּ הֵשַׁמּוּ.

שְׁפָךְ עֲלֵיהֶם זַעְמֶךָ וַחֲרוֹן אַפְּךָ יַשִּׂיגֵם.

תִּרְדוֹף בְּאַף וְתַשְׁמִידֵם מִתַּחַת שְׁמֵי יהוה.

Pour out Your wrath upon those who do not know You and upon the governments which do not call upon Your name. For they have devoured Jacob and laid waste his dwelling place (Psalms 79:6–7).

Pour out Your fury upon them,
let the fierceness of Your anger
overtake them (Psalms 69:25).

Pursue them in indignation and destroy them
from under Your heavens (Lamentations 3:66).

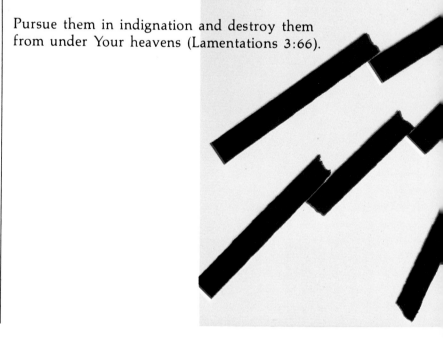

102

I will send the prophet Elijah to you. When his days on earth had run their tumultuous course, the Prophet Elijah was translated to heaven in a chariot of fire. Yet many are certain that Eliahu never left us. The "Bird of Heaven" dons different guises in his variegated role as companion and protector of his people, and legion are the legends of his miraculous meditation on behalf of the poor and the persecuted. But his most important mission is still to be accomplished. For he is the herald of the messianic era. Tradition places the Pesaḥ of the future like the Pesaḥ in the past in Nisan, the month of *nisim* (miracles). So we fling wide our doors for his visitations, hoping that this year the age-old reverie will become reality, that the elusive Elijah will finally drink from his cup . . . and proclaim the long awaited Messiah. Some families greet the unseen visitor with a hearty, *Barukh haba,* welcome!"

Opening the door. The custom is venerable, misted in metaphor, history and messianic speculation. Was the door opened as a reminder that the gates of Mitzrayim (from which no slave has ever escaped!) were unlocked for us? Were kindly hosts on the lookout for strangers or tardy guests? Were wary celebrants on guard against informers or against malevolent neighbors plotting devilry? Were Jews, even when the forces of evil were arrayed against them, opening their doors (thereby rendering themselves even more assailable) to prove their faith in the guardianship of God, who would neither slumber nor sleep on this "night of watching"? In comparatively recent times, the practice became associated with Elijah. Certainly, this is a night of openness, as we open our minds to new understanding, new revelations, new possibilities for growth.

הִנֵּה אָנֹכִי שֹׁלֵחַ לָכֶם אֵת אֵלִיָּה הַנָּבִיא לִפְנֵי בּוֹא יוֹם יהוה הַגָּדוֹל וְהַנּוֹרָא, וְהֵשִׁיב לֵב אָבוֹת עַל בָּנִים וְלֵב בָּנִים עַל אֲבוֹתָם.

"Behold, before the coming of the great and awesome day of Adonai, I will send the prophet Elijah to you. He will turn the hearts of the parents to the children and the hearts of the children to their parents" (Malachi 3:23–24).

Elijah the Prophet

The Fifth Cup of the evening belongs to Elijah. The first four cups represent four landmarks on the road to redemption; for God lightened our burdens, removed our burdens, took us out of Mitzrayim and made us His people. Yet the Bible speaks of a fifth landmark: our resettlement in the land of our ancestors. For centuries, while our land languished in foster care, the Fifth Cup reminded us of Elijah's promised coming and our promised inheritance. Today Israel is ours again. A homeless people has been restored to its cherished homeland. Jerusalem, never forgotten in the bleak black night of exile, is once more our capital. And the Cup of Elijah is the Cup of Redemption . . . in anticipation of the redemption that will bring enduring peace.

לָכֵן הִנֵּה יָמִים בָּאִים, נְאֻם יהוה, וְלֹא יֵאָמֵר עוֹד חַי יהוה אֲשֶׁר הֶעֱלָה אֶת בְּנֵי יִשְׂרָאֵל מֵאֶרֶץ מִצְרָיִם, כִּי אִם חַי יהוה אֲשֶׁר הֶעֱלָה אֶת בְּנֵי יִשְׂרָאֵל מֵאֶרֶץ צָפוֹן וּמִכֹּל הָאֲרָצוֹת אֲשֶׁר הִדִּיחָם שָׁמָּה, וַהֲשִׁבֹתִים עַל אַדְמָתָם אֲשֶׁר נָתַתִּי לַאֲבוֹתָם.

"Behold the days are coming, says Adonai, when it shall no more be said, 'As Adonai lives, who brought the people Israel out of the land of Mitzrayim'; but, 'As Adonai lives who brought the people Israel from the land of the north and from all the lands into which He had driven them'; and I will bring them back into their land that I gave to their ancestors" (Jeremiah 16:14–15).

Earlier in the Seder we recited the four biblical verses (Deuteronomy 26:5–8) that summarize the Exodus experience. Now we recite the fifth verse (Deuteronomy 26:9) that celebrates a crowning facet of that experience: our homecoming.

וַיְבִאֵנוּ אֶל הַמָּקוֹם הַזֶּה, וַיִּתֶּן לָנוּ אֶת הָאָרֶץ הַזֹּאת, אֶרֶץ זָבַת חָלָב וּדְבָשׁ.

"And He brought us to this place and gave us this land, a land flowing with milk and honey" (Deuteronomy 26:9).

אֵלִיָּהוּ הַנָּבִיא, אֵלִיָּהוּ הַתִּשְׁבִּי, אֵלִיָּהוּ, אֵלִיָּהוּ, אֵלִיָּהוּ הַגִּלְעָדִי, בִּמְהֵרָה בְיָמֵינוּ יָבֹא אֵלֵינוּ עִם מָשִׁיחַ בֶּן דָּוִד.

Soon, in our days, the prophet Elijah
will come, bringing the Messiah.

Eliyahu hanavi, Eliyahu hatishbi,
Eliyahu, Eliyahu, Eliyahu hagiladi.
Bimheirah b'yameinu yavo eileinu,
Im Mashiaḥ ben David, im Mashiaḥ ben David.

Close the door and be seated.
Elijah's cup remains on the table as we rejoice, in psalm and song, for past redemptions and for the future redemption soon to dawn upon us.

The prophet Elijah. For a hundred generations from his time until our own, Elijah the Gileadite, uncompromising exponent of the prophetic traditions of the simple life and simple worship, has continued to haunt our imagination. Within a few decades he became a legend. While those who had seen and known him were still alive, his activity came to be described in impossible hyperbole which obscured, when it did not destroy, the historical personality. Great leader, thinker and statesman who for a generation had single-handedly held the forces of ethical and religious disintegration in check . . . seen in the light of the social conditions of his day, Elijah emerges as one of the supreme geniuses of western history.

The question of the Fifth Cup. The Four Cups, as noted earlier, mark the first four promises enumerated in Exodus 6:6–8: "I will free you, I will deliver you, I will redeem you, I will take you to be My people, I will bring you to your land." However, some authorities were of the opinion that a fifth cup should mark the fifth promise contained in this passage. Since the Rabbis could not resolve this problem to their satisfaction, they decided on an ingenious compromise: we pour the fifth cup but we do not drink it. We leave it for Elijah. So, in addition to bringing advance word of the Messiah, Elijah will also bring the answers to questions that have perplexed us for ages. A people compulsively prone to answering a question with a question, we have yet another reason to welcome the prophet with all the answers.

For Zion's sake I will not keep silent,
    and for Jerusalem's sake I will not rest,
until her vindication goes forth as brightness,
    and her salvation as a flaming torch.
You shall be a crown of beauty in the hand of Adonai,
    and a royal diadem in the palm of your God.
You shall no more be termed "Forsaken,"
    and your land shall no more be termed "Desolate";
but you shall be called "I delight in her,"
    and as a bridegroom rejoices over his bride,
so shall your God rejoice over you (Isaiah 62:1,3–4,5).

I believe that a wondrous breed of Jews will spring up from the earth. The Maccabees will rise again. The Jews who will it shall achieve their own State. We shall live at last as free men and women on our own soil, and in our own homes die peacefully. The world will be liberated by our freedom, enriched by our wealth, magnified by our greatness. And whatever we attempt there for our own benefit will redound mightily and beneficially to the good of all mankind.

Theodor Herzl

The land of Israel is part of the very essence of our nationhood; it is bound organically to its very life and inner being. Human reason, even at its most sublime, cannot begin to understand the unique holiness of *Eretz Yisrael*. Deep in the heart of every Jew, in its purest and holiest recesses, love for this land blazes like the fire on the altar of the Temple, burning unceasingly, with a steady flame. . . . Within the Jewish people as a whole, this is the living source of its desire for freedom, of its longing for a life worthy of the name, of its hope for redemption, of the striving toward a full, uncontradictory and unbounded Jewish life. This is the meaning of the Jewish people's undying love for *Eretz Yisrael*—the Land of Holiness, the Land of God.

Rabbi Abraham Isaac Kook

The wilderness and the parched land shall be glad;
    the desert shall burst into blossom.
It shall flower abundantly and rejoice,
    even with joy and with song,
    sharing the glory of Lebanon,
    the splendor of Carmel and Sharon.
They shall see the glory of Adonai,
    the splendor of our God.
And the ransomed of Adonai shall return,
    and come with singing unto Zion,
    crowned with everlasting joy (Isaiah 35:1–2,10).

Hallel, which is followed by the songs which start on page 118, concludes with the Fourth Cup (page 134) and Nirtzah.

כִּי לְשִׁמְךָ תֵּן כָּבוֹד   לֹא לָנוּ יהוה לֹא לָנוּ

עַל חַסְדְּךָ עַל אֲמִתֶּךָ.

אַיֵּה נָא אֱלֹהֵיהֶם.   לָמָּה יֹאמְרוּ הַגּוֹיִם

כֹּל אֲשֶׁר חָפֵץ עָשָׂה.   וֵאלֹהֵינוּ בַשָּׁמָיִם

מַעֲשֵׂה יְדֵי אָדָם.   עֲצַבֵּיהֶם כֶּסֶף וְזָהָב

עֵינַיִם לָהֶם וְלֹא יִרְאוּ.   פֶּה לָהֶם וְלֹא יְדַבֵּרוּ,

אַף לָהֶם וְלֹא יְרִיחוּן.   אָזְנַיִם לָהֶם וְלֹא יִשְׁמָעוּ,

רַגְלֵיהֶם וְלֹא יְהַלֵּכוּ   יְדֵיהֶם וְלֹא יְמִישׁוּן

לֹא יֶהְגּוּ בִּגְרוֹנָם.

כֹּל אֲשֶׁר בֹּטֵחַ בָּהֶם.   כְּמוֹהֶם יִהְיוּ עֹשֵׂיהֶם

עֶזְרָם וּמָגִנָּם הוּא.   יִשְׂרָאֵל בְּטַח בַּיהוה

עֶזְרָם וּמָגִנָּם הוּא.   בֵּית אַהֲרֹן בִּטְחוּ בַיהוה

עֶזְרָם וּמָגִנָּם הוּא.   יִרְאֵי יהוה בִּטְחוּ בַיהוה

Not for us. Why did the Revelation take place in the wilderness, in a veritable no-man's land? Perhaps to indicate that the Torah was potentially everyman's land, that all were welcome to dwell within its all-embracing borders and to drink of its living waters. In Temple times the priests would offer prayers for all the nations of the world, and in the darkest of dark ages Israel never relinquished the dazzling daydream of the time when all roads would lead to Zion and the God of the universe would be universally acknowledged and acclaimed.

Whatever He wills. God is all-powerful and all-knowing but neither His omnipotence nor His omniscience impinge on human freedom. Setting before us good and evil, life and death, God exhorts us to choose life. The choice is ours, for everything is in the hands of heaven ... except the fear of heaven. Maimonides spells it out: "Each of us can become upright like our teacher Moses or wicked like Jeroboam, wise or foolish, kindly or cruel, churlish or charitable, and so on. There is no coercion. Each of us wittingly selects the path we please to pursue. Hence we will be judged for our deeds, according to our deeds."

יְבָרֵךְ אֶת בֵּית יִשְׂרָאֵל   יהוה זְכָרָנוּ יְבָרֵךְ

יְבָרֵךְ אֶת בֵּית אַהֲרֹן.

הַקְּטַנִּים עִם הַגְּדֹלִים.   יְבָרֵךְ יִרְאֵי יהוה

עֲלֵיכֶם וְעַל בְּנֵיכֶם.   יֹסֵף יהוה עֲלֵיכֶם

עֹשֵׂה שָׁמַיִם וָאָרֶץ.   בְּרוּכִים אַתֶּם לַיהוה

וְהָאָרֶץ נָתַן לִבְנֵי אָדָם.   הַשָּׁמַיִם שָׁמַיִם לַיהוה

וְלֹא כָּל יֹרְדֵי דוּמָה.   לֹא הַמֵּתִים יְהַלְלוּ יָהּ

מֵעַתָּה וְעַד עוֹלָם. הַלְלוּיָהּ.   וַאֲנַחְנוּ נְבָרֵךְ יָהּ

Their idols. "It is the object of the whole Torah to abolish idolatry and utterly uproot it, and to demolish the belief that the stars can interfere, for good or evil, in human affairs." Those who hitch their wagons to the stars are self-delivered hostages to fortune, marionettes who allow their minds and their movements to be manipulated. Keying their conduct to the uncaring constellations, they trade dynamism for domination, freedom for fatalistic quiescence. They are perpetually prisoners in the confines of an astrological Mitzrayim.

Their idols are silver and gold. Nowadays no one admits to bowing to Baal or sacrificing to Mammon. Yet an idol by any other name is still an idol. Slavish conformity to society, mindless pursuit of success, submission to the thralldom of *things*—such forms of idol worship are all too prevalent. The Rabbis equated idolatry with hatred, pride, anger, avarice, slander and hypocrisy, and these notoriously durable pseudo-deities have yet to be dethroned.

The earth He entrusted to mortals. "The heavens are already heavenly," observes Rabbi Ḥanokh of Alexander, "but the earth has been consigned to us so that we might make it more like heaven." When we enjoy our planet's plenty, and in benedictions acknowledge the origin of our enjoyment, then we inherit the earth.

Hallel

Hallel, which is followed by the songs which start on page 118, concludes with the Fourth Cup (page 135) and Nirtzah.

Not for us, Adonai, not for us but for Yourself
win praise through Your love and faithfulness.
    Why should the nations say: "Where is their God?"
Our God is in heaven; He does whatever He wills.
    Their idols are silver and gold,
    made by human hands.
They have a mouth and cannot speak,
eyes and cannot see.
    They have ears and cannot hear,
    a nose and cannot smell.
They have hands and cannot feel, feet and cannot walk;
    They cannot make a sound in their throat.
Their makers shall become like them;
so shall all who trust in them.
    Let the House of Israel trust in Adonai;
    He is their help and their shield.
Let the House of Aaron trust in Adonai;
He is their help and their shield.
    Let those who revere Adonai trust in Adonai;
    He is their help and their shield.
                                        (Psalms 115:1–11)

Adonai remembers us with blessings.
He will bless the House of Israel.
    He will bless the House of Aaron.
He will bless those who revere Him,
young and old alike.
    May Adonai increase your blessings,
    yours and your children's as well.
May you be blessed by Adonai,
Maker of heaven and earth.
    The heavens belong to Adonai,
    and the earth He has entrusted to mortals.
The dead cannot praise Adonai,
nor can those who go down into silence.
    But we shall praise Adonai now and forever.
    Halleluyah!   (Psalms 115:12–18)

אָהַבְתִּי כִּי יִשְׁמַע יהוה אֶת קוֹלִי תַּחֲנוּנָי.

כִּי הִטָּה אָזְנוֹ לִי וּבְיָמַי אֶקְרָא.

אֲפָפוּנִי חֶבְלֵי מָוֶת וּמְצָרֵי שְׁאוֹל מְצָאוּנִי

צָרָה וְיָגוֹן אֶמְצָא.

וּבְשֵׁם יהוה אֶקְרָא אָנָּה יהוה מַלְּטָה נַפְשִׁי.

חַנּוּן יהוה וְצַדִּיק וֵאלֹהֵינוּ מְרַחֵם.

שֹׁמֵר פְּתָאִים יהוה דַּלּוֹתִי וְלִי יְהוֹשִׁיעַ.

שׁוּבִי נַפְשִׁי לִמְנוּחָיְכִי כִּי יהוה גָּמַל עָלָיְכִי.

כִּי חִלַּצְתָּ נַפְשִׁי מִמָּוֶת אֶת עֵינִי מִן דִּמְעָה

אֶת רַגְלִי מִדֶּחִי.

אֶתְהַלֵּךְ לִפְנֵי יהוה בְּאַרְצוֹת הַחַיִּים.

הֶאֱמַנְתִּי כִּי אֲדַבֵּר אֲנִי עָנִיתִי מְאֹד.

אֲנִי אָמַרְתִּי בְחָפְזִי כָּל הָאָדָם כֹּזֵב.

מָה אָשִׁיב לַיהוה כָּל תַּגְמוּלוֹהִי עָלָי.

כּוֹס יְשׁוּעוֹת אֶשָּׂא וּבְשֵׁם יהוה אֶקְרָא.

נְדָרַי לַיהוה אֲשַׁלֵּם נֶגְדָה נָּא לְכָל עַמּוֹ.

יָקָר בְּעֵינֵי יהוה הַמָּוְתָה לַחֲסִידָיו.

אָנָּה יהוה כִּי אֲנִי עַבְדֶּךָ אֲנִי עַבְדְּךָ בֶּן אֲמָתֶךָ

פִּתַּחְתָּ לְמוֹסֵרָי.

לְךָ אֶזְבַּח זֶבַח תּוֹדָה וּבְשֵׁם יהוה אֶקְרָא.

נְדָרַי לַיהוה אֲשַׁלֵּם נֶגְדָה נָּא לְכָל עַמּוֹ.

בְּחַצְרוֹת בֵּית יהוה בְּתוֹכֵכִי יְרוּשָׁלָיִם. הַלְלוּיָהּ.

Hallel is part of the liturgy on all major festivals, yet on the last six days of *Pesaḥ*, we recite only an abbreviated form. Why this curious curtailment of rejoicing on this most joyful *yom tov?* The rationale lies deep in the psyche of the Jewish people, in its instinctive empathy with suffering, its inability to exult over vanquished enemies. Just as we diminish the wine in our cups when we recall the plagues visited upon the obdurate Egyptians, because our happiness is diminished by their discomfiture (albeit well-merited), so we follow the example of the angelic choir at the Sea of Reeds and we subdue our song.

As General Yitzhak Rabin commented after the Six-Day War: "The joy of our soldiers is incomplete, and their celebrations are marred by sorrow and shock. There are some who abstain from all celebration. The men in the front lines saw with their own eyes not only the glory of victory but also the price of victory: their comrades fallen beside them soaked in blood. The terrible price paid by our enemies touched the hearts of many of our men as well. It may be that the Jewish people has never learned and never accustomed itself to feel the triumph of conquest and victory, and we receive it with mixed feelings."

Adonai listens. Only Israel has understood that the real God is the God whom we can address because He is the God who addresses us. At God's word the world came into being. Creation is a response. Life is a dialogue. The question is man. The answer is God.

108

Delivered from death? We are God's memory and the heart of mankind. We do not always know this, but the others do, and that is why they treat us with suspicion and cruelty. Memory frightens them. Through us they are linked to the beginning and the end. By eliminating us they hope to gain immortality. But, in truth, it is not given us to die, not even if we wanted to. We cannot die, because we are the question.

All men are false. The Torah commands us to be truthful to one another. It is just as important, says the Yehudi, the Holy Jew of Pshiskhah, for us to be truthful to ourselves.

Grievous in the sight of Adonai. God desires the destruction of sin, not the destruction of sinners. "I have no pleasure in the death of the wicked!" (Ezekiel 33:11). If He grieves at the death of ungodly ones, how much more so must He grieve over the death of those who love and serve Him?

You have released me from bondage. But have we released ourselves from the bonds of materialism? Have we learned how to prevent license from becoming licentiousness? "No man is free," remark the Rabbis, "unless he occupies himself with the study of Torah."

In the presence of all the people. It is not enough to be Jewish in the privacy of our own homes. We must stand up and be counted, openly identifying ourselves with our brothers and sisters, upholding in public the honor of the Jewish people. The term *Yisrael*, as Rabbi Max Kadushin points out, applies to both the individual Jew and to Jewry as a whole. So who is the "wicked child"? He who separates himself from the community.

I love to know that Adonai listens
to my cry of supplication.
  Because He gives me a hearing,
  I will call on Him all my days.
The cords of death encompassed me,
the grave held me in its grip;
I found myself in anguish and despair.
  I called on Adonai,
  I prayed that He would save me.
Gracious is Adonai, and just;
our God is compassionate.
  Adonai protects the simple;
  I was brought low and He saved me.
Be at ease once again, my soul,
for Adonai has dealt kindly with you.
  He has delivered me from death,
  my eyes from tears, my feet from stumbling.
I shall walk before Adonai in the land of the living.
  I kept my faith even when greatly afflicted,
  even when I cried out in panic, "All men are false!"

(Psalms 116:1–11)

How can I repay Adonai for all His gifts to me?
  I will raise the cup of deliverance,
  and invoke Adonai by name.
I will pay my vows to Adonai
in the presence of all His people.
  Grievous in the sight of Adonai
  is the death of His faithful.
I am Your servant, born of Your maidservant;
You have released me from bondage.
  To You will I bring an offering,
  and invoke Adonai by name.
I will pay my vows to Adonai
in the presence of all His people,
in the courts of the house of Adonai,
in the midst of Jerusalem. Halleluyah!

(Psalms 116:12–19)

הַלְלוּ אֶת יהוה כָּל גּוֹיִם   שַׁבְּחוּהוּ כָּל הָאֻמִּים.
כִּי גָבַר עָלֵינוּ חַסְדּוֹ   וֶאֱמֶת יהוה לְעוֹלָם. הַלְלוּיָהּ.

הוֹדוּ לַיהוה כִּי טוֹב   כִּי לְעוֹלָם חַסְדּוֹ.
יֹאמַר נָא יִשְׂרָאֵל   כִּי לְעוֹלָם חַסְדּוֹ.
יֹאמְרוּ נָא בֵית אַהֲרֹן   כִּי לְעוֹלָם חַסְדּוֹ.
יֹאמְרוּ נָא יִרְאֵי יהוה   כִּי לְעוֹלָם חַסְדּוֹ.

מִן הַמֵּצַר קָרָאתִי יָּהּ   עָנָנִי בַמֶּרְחָב יָהּ.
יהוה לִי לֹא אִירָא   מַה יַּעֲשֶׂה לִי אָדָם.
יהוה לִי בְּעֹזְרָי   וַאֲנִי אֶרְאֶה בְשֹׂנְאָי.
טוֹב לַחֲסוֹת בַּיהוה   מִבְּטֹחַ בָּאָדָם.
טוֹב לַחֲסוֹת בַּיהוה   מִבְּטֹחַ בִּנְדִיבִים.
כָּל גּוֹיִם סְבָבוּנִי   בְּשֵׁם יהוה כִּי אֲמִילַם.
סַבּוּנִי גַם סְבָבוּנִי   בְּשֵׁם יהוה כִּי אֲמִילַם.
סַבּוּנִי כִדְבֹרִים   דֹּעֲכוּ כְּאֵשׁ קוֹצִים
בְּשֵׁם יהוה כִּי אֲמִילַם.
דָּחֹה דְחִיתַנִי לִנְפֹּל   וַיהוה עֲזָרָנִי.
עָזִּי וְזִמְרָת יָהּ   וַיְהִי לִי לִישׁוּעָה.
קוֹל רִנָּה וִישׁוּעָה   בְּאָהֳלֵי צַדִּיקִים
יְמִין יהוה עֹשָׂה חָיִל.
יְמִין יהוה רוֹמֵמָה   יְמִין יהוה עֹשָׂה חָיִל.
לֹא אָמוּת כִּי אֶחְיֶה   וַאֲסַפֵּר מַעֲשֵׂי יָהּ.

Praise Adonai. This short psalm, the shortest in the psalter, takes the long view, looking ahead to the time when all the inhabitants of the world, caught up in messianic momentum, will accept the yoke of the kingdom and join us in worshipping the King of kings.

His love. "The most noteworthy day in history," declares Rabbi Akiva, "was the day on which the Song of Songs was composed. All the books of the Scripture are holy, but this one is the Holy of Holies." Why does he speak of *shir hashirim* in these exalted terms? Because he views it as a garland of hymns, fashioned in honor of the mystical marriage of God and Israel. Such a view is true to biblical imagery. For the prophets often used the rhapsodic language of romantic love. "I will betroth you to Me forever. I will betroth you to Me in righteousness and in justice, in love and in compassion. I will betroth you to Me in faithfulness, and you shall know Adonai" (Hosea, 2:21–22). This, incontrovertibly, was a marriage made in heaven.

He answered by setting me free. What was Israel's response to freedom? When Israel came forth from bondage, it was not simply to enjoy liberty but to make liberty an instrument of service. The prophet Amos reminds us that the Philistines came forth from Crete and the Arameans from Kir, much as the Israelites came forth from Mitzrayim. But none of these peoples have left records interpreting their liberations as a means to a higher end. The Israelites alone made the moment of their origin as a people one of permanent self-dedication to the principle of universal freedom as the essential prerequisite for spiritual growth. Hence the event has meaning for all time and for all living peoples.

110

Adonai has set us free. When He brought us to Sinai, He brought us to freedom. When Moses came down from the heights with the tablets of the Law, "the tablets were the work of God, and the writing was the writing of God, graven upon the tablets." The Rabbis comment, "for *harut* (graven) read *herut* (freedom)" (*Avot* 6:2), for they regard law and liberty as synonymous.

They surrounded me. Why is this phrase repeated so many times? Because we have been surrounded so many times by feral adversaries. Because we have found ourselves so many times in surroundings grown suddenly inimical, menacing, malign. Only with God as our help and our shield have we been able to survive these sanguinary encirclements.

I shall not die but live. In the aftermath of the Holocaust, Jewish survival has acquired a new dimension: a dimension of sanctity. Jewish survival after Auschwitz is a sacred testimony to all mankind that life and love, not death and hatred, shall prevail. This may be an age without heroes. It is, however, the heroic age *par excellence* in all of Jewish history. . . . Nowhere is this truth as unmistakable as in the State of Israel. The State of Israel is collectively what the survivor is individually—testimony on behalf of all mankind to life against death, to sanity against madness, to Jewish self-affirmation against every form of flight from it and to the God of the ancient covenant against all lapses into paganism. . . Its watchword is *Am Yisrael hai*—the people Israel *lives*.

Praise Adonai, all nations.
Laud Him, all peoples.
　　His love has overwhelmed us,
　　His faithfulness endures forever. Halleluyah!

(Psalm 117)

Give thanks to Adonai for He is good;
His love endures forever.
　　Let the House of Israel declare:
　　His love endures forever.
Let the House of Aaron declare:
His love endures forever.
　　Let those who revere Adonai declare:
　　His love endures forever.

In my distress I called to Adonai;
He answered by setting me free.
　　Adonai is with me, I shall not fear;
　　what can mortals do to me?
With Adonai at my side, as my help,
I will yet see the fall of my foes.
　　Better to depend on Adonai
　　than to trust in mortals;
Better to depend on Adonai than to trust in nobility.
　　Though all nations surrounded me,
　　in Adonai's name I overcame them.
Though they surrounded and encircled me,
in Adonai's name I overcame them.
　　Though they surrounded me like bees,
　　they were snuffed out like burning thorns;
In Adonai's name I overcame them.
　　Hard pressed was I, I nearly fell,
　　but Adonai helped me.
Adonai is my strength, my song, my deliverance.
　　The homes of the righteous echo
　　with songs of deliverance:
"The might of Adonai is triumphant;
　　the might of Adonai is supreme;
　　the might of Adonai is triumphant."
I shall not die but live to tell the deeds of Adonai.

111

I thank You. The very first words of praise recorded in the Bible issued from the lips of Leah, gratified mother of six of Jacob's sons.

וְלַמָּוֶת לֹא נְתָנָנִי.   יַסֹּר יִסְּרַנִּי יָּה

אָבֹא בָם אוֹדֶה יָּה.   פִּתְחוּ לִי שַׁעֲרֵי צֶדֶק

צַדִּיקִים יָבֹאוּ בוֹ.   זֶה הַשַּׁעַר לַיהוה

Deliver us, Adonai! And when the people saw a great multitude of the enemy's hosts, they said, "How shall we be able, being so few, to fight against so many?" Judah answered, "Victory in battle does not depend on the size of the armies, but strength comes from God. They come against us in much pride and iniquity to destroy us. But we fight for our lives and our Torah. Be not afraid. Remember how our ancestors were saved at the Sea of Reeds when Pharaoh and his horsemen pursued them. Let us implore God to remember His covenant with our families and to overthrow our foes. Then all the nations will know that there is One who protects and saves Israel." And Judah led them into battle, and fought like a lion, and behold, the enemy forces were vanquished and they fled. And Israel had a great deliverance, and sang songs of thanksgiving, and praised God for His goodness, because His mercy endures forever.

The year 164 B.C.E. saw history's first recorded fight for freedom of worship. When Antiochus Epiphanes of Syria attempted to crush Judaism and impose his own brand of paganism upon us, the priest Mattathias and his sons led the call to arms. Against overwhelming odds, the Maccabees recaptured Jerusalem, rededicated the Temple, and proclaimed an independent Judea. At Hanukkah, as at Pesah, we celebrate the victory of right over might, conscience over cohorts, freedom over tyranny, light over darkness.

Repeat each of the following four verses.

וַתְּהִי לִי לִישׁוּעָה.   אוֹדְךָ כִּי עֲנִיתָנִי

הָיְתָה לְרֹאשׁ פִּנָּה.   אֶבֶן מָאֲסוּ הַבּוֹנִים

הִיא נִפְלָאת בְּעֵינֵינוּ.   מֵאֵת יהוה הָיְתָה זֹּאת

נָגִילָה וְנִשְׂמְחָה בוֹ.   זֶה הַיּוֹם עָשָׂה יהוה

אָנָּא יהוה הוֹשִׁיעָה נָּא.   אָנָּא יהוה הוֹשִׁיעָה נָּא.

אָנָּא יהוה הַצְלִיחָה נָא.   אָנָּא יהוה הַצְלִיחָה נָא.

Repeat each of the following four verses.

בֵּרַכְנוּכֶם מִבֵּית יהוה.   בָּרוּךְ הַבָּא בְּשֵׁם יהוה

אִסְרוּ חַג בַּעֲבֹתִים עַד קַרְנוֹת הַמִּזְבֵּחַ.   אֵל יהוה וַיָּאֶר לָנוּ

אֱלֹהַי אֲרוֹמְמֶךָּ.   אֵלִי אַתָּה וְאוֹדֶךָ

כִּי לְעוֹלָם חַסְדּוֹ.   הוֹדוּ לַיהוה כִּי טוֹב

יְהַלְלוּךָ יהוה אֱלֹהֵינוּ כָּל מַעֲשֶׂיךָ וַחֲסִידֶיךָ צַדִּיקִים עוֹשֵׂי רְצוֹנֶךָ וְכָל עַמְּךָ בֵּית יִשְׂרָאֵל, בְּרִנָּה יוֹדוּ וִיבָרְכוּ וִישַׁבְּחוּ וִיפָאֲרוּ וִירוֹמְמוּ וְיַעֲרִיצוּ וְיַקְדִּישׁוּ וְיַמְלִיכוּ אֶת שִׁמְךָ מַלְכֵּנוּ. כִּי לְךָ טוֹב לְהוֹדוֹת וּלְשִׁמְךָ נָאֶה לְזַמֵּר, כִּי מֵעוֹלָם וְעַד עוֹלָם אַתָּה אֵל. בָּרוּךְ אַתָּה יהוה מֶלֶךְ מְהֻלָּל בַּתִּשְׁבָּחוֹת.

The righteous shall enter. And who are "the righteous"? They are Godfearing men and women of all nations. The founders of ecumenism, Israel's seers and sages, combined partiality towards their people with a pan-oramic vista that encompassed all people. One Rabbi, with a uni-versalism unmatched in Judaism's daughter religions, enunciated this supra-chauvinistic credo: "I call heaven and earth to witness that whether they be Gentile or Jew, man or woman, servant or handmaid, according to the deeds they do, so will be their judgment and their recompense." And in eighteenth century Poland, in a climate unconducive to religious tolerance, the Maggid of Kozhe-nitz would pray for redemption in these touching terms: "Master of the Universe, redeem Israel, I implore You. Israel deserves to be redeemed. But if the time for their redemption is not nigh, then redeem the other nations, and redeem them soon."

You are my God. Nothing less than a good old honest heathen pantheon would satisfy the crazes and cravings of our present pampered humanity, with its pagan reminiscences, its meta-physical confusion of languages and theological idiosyncracies. True religion is above these demands. It is not a jack-of-all-trades, meaning monotheism to the philosopher, pluralism to the crowd, some mysterious Nothing to the agnostic, pantheism to the poet, service of man to the hero-worshipper. Its mission is just as much to teach the world that there *are* false gods as to bring it nearer to the true one. Abraham, the friend of God, who was des-tined to become the first winner of souls, began his career, according to the legend, with breaking idols, and it is his particular glory to have been in opposition to the whole world.

Adonai severely chastened me,
but He did not doom me to death.
Open for me the gates of triumph,
that I may enter and thank Adonai.
This is the gateway of Adonai;
the righteous shall enter through it.

(Psalms 118:1–20)

Repeat each of the following four verses.

I thank You for having answered me;
You have become my deliverance.
The stone which the builders rejected
has become the corner-stone.
This is Adonai's doing;
it is marvelous in our sight.
This is the day Adonai has made;
let us exult and rejoice in it.
Deliver us, Adonai, we implore You.
Ana adonai, hoshiah na.
Prosper us, Adonai, we implore You.
Ana adonai, hatzliḥah na.

Repeat each of the following four verses.

Blessed in the name of Adonai are all who come;
We bless you from the house of Adonai.
Adonai is God who has given us light.
Wreathe with myrtle the festive procession
as it winds its way to the altar.
You are my God, and I thank You.
You are my God, and I exalt You.
Give thanks to Adonai, for He is good;
His love endures forever.

(Psalms 118:21–29)

May all creation praise You, Adonai our God. May the pious, the righteous who do Your will and all Your people, the House of Israel, join in thanking You with joyous song. May they praise, revere, adore, extol, exalt and sanctify Your sovereign glory, our King. To You it is good to give thanks; to Your glory it is fitting to sing. From age to age, everlastingly You are God. Praised are You, Adonai, King acclaimed with songs of praise.

נִשְׁמַת

נִשְׁמַת כָּל חַי תְּבָרֵךְ אֶת שִׁמְךָ יהוה אֱלֹהֵינוּ, וְרוּחַ כָּל בָּשָׂר תְּפָאֵר וּתְרוֹמֵם זִכְרְךָ מַלְכֵּנוּ תָּמִיד. מִן הָעוֹלָם וְעַד הָעוֹלָם אַתָּה אֵל, וּמִבַּלְעָדֶיךָ אֵין לָנוּ מֶלֶךְ גּוֹאֵל וּמוֹשִׁיעַ, פּוֹדֶה וּמַצִּיל וּמְפַרְנֵס וּמְרַחֵם בְּכָל עֵת צָרָה וְצוּקָה. אֵין לָנוּ מֶלֶךְ אֶלָּא אָתָּה. אֱלֹהֵי הָרִאשׁוֹנִים וְהָאַחֲרוֹנִים, אֱלוֹהַּ כָּל בְּרִיּוֹת. אֲדוֹן כָּל תּוֹלָדוֹת, הַמְהֻלָּל בְּרֹב הַתִּשְׁבָּחוֹת, הַמְנַהֵג עוֹלָמוֹ בְּחֶסֶד וּבְרִיּוֹתָיו בְּרַחֲמִים. וַיהוה לֹא יָנוּם וְלֹא יִישָׁן, הַמְעוֹרֵר יְשֵׁנִים, וְהַמֵּקִיץ נִרְדָּמִים, וְהַמֵּשִׂיחַ אִלְּמִים, וְהַמַּתִּיר אֲסוּרִים, וְהַסּוֹמֵךְ נוֹפְלִים, וְהַזּוֹקֵף כְּפוּפִים, לְךָ לְבַדְּךָ אֲנַחְנוּ מוֹדִים.

אִלּוּ פִינוּ מָלֵא שִׁירָה כַּיָּם
וּלְשׁוֹנֵנוּ רִנָּה כַּהֲמוֹן גַּלָּיו
וְשִׂפְתוֹתֵינוּ שֶׁבַח כְּמֶרְחֲבֵי רָקִיעַ
וְעֵינֵינוּ מְאִירוֹת כַּשֶּׁמֶשׁ וְכַיָּרֵחַ
וְיָדֵינוּ פְרוּשׂוֹת כְּנִשְׁרֵי שָׁמָיִם
וְרַגְלֵינוּ קַלּוֹת כָּאַיָּלוֹת
אֵין אֲנַחְנוּ מַסְפִּיקִים לְהוֹדוֹת לְךָ, יהוה אֱלֹהֵינוּ וֵאלֹהֵי אֲבוֹתֵינוּ, וּלְבָרֵךְ אֶת שִׁמְךָ עַל אַחַת מֵאֶלֶף אַלְפֵי אֲלָפִים וְרִבֵּי רְבָבוֹת פְּעָמִים הַטּוֹבוֹת שֶׁעָשִׂיתָ עִם אֲבוֹתֵינוּ וְעִמָּנוּ.

מִמִּצְרַיִם גְּאַלְתָּנוּ, יהוה אֱלֹהֵינוּ, וּמִבֵּית עֲבָדִים פְּדִיתָנוּ, בְּרָעָב זַנְתָּנוּ, וּבְשָׂבָע כִּלְכַּלְתָּנוּ, מֵחֶרֶב הִצַּלְתָּנוּ, וּמִדֶּבֶר מִלַּטְתָּנוּ, וּמֵחֳלָיִם רָעִים וְנֶאֱמָנִים דִּלִּיתָנוּ. עַד הֵנָּה עֲזָרוּנוּ רַחֲמֶיךָ, וְלֹא עֲזָבוּנוּ חֲסָדֶיךָ, וְאַל תִּטְּשֵׁנוּ, יהוה אֱלֹהֵינוּ, לָנֶצַח. עַל כֵּן, אֵבָרִים שֶׁפִּלַּגְתָּ בָּנוּ, וְרוּחַ וּנְשָׁמָה שֶׁנָּפַחְתָּ בְּאַפֵּינוּ, וְלָשׁוֹן אֲשֶׁר שַׂמְתָּ בְּפִינוּ, הֵן הֵם יוֹדוּ וִיבָרְכוּ וִישַׁבְּחוּ וִיפָאֲרוּ וִירוֹמְמוּ וְיַעֲרִיצוּ וְיַקְדִּישׁוּ וְיַמְלִיכוּ אֶת שִׁמְךָ מַלְכֵּנוּ, כִּי כָל פֶּה לְךָ יוֹדֶה, וְכָל לָשׁוֹן לְךָ תִּשָּׁבַע,

Nishmat

Some passages of *Nishmat* are as old as the Temple, as old as the Talmud. Authorship is obscure, variously attributed to different personages, among them Shimon ben Shetaḥ, statesman-scholar of the Hasmonean era. Every Shabbat and every yom tov, this soaring rhapsody of prayer and praise is recited in the synagogue. And one day it will be recited everywhere, as people of all faiths join us in good faith in extolling the God of all creation.

The breath of all that lives praises You, Adonai, our God. The force that drives all flesh exalts You, our King, always. Transcending space and time, You are God. Without You we have no other to rescue and redeem us, to save us and sustain us, to show us mercy in disaster and distress. God of all ages, God of all creatures, ceaselessly extolled, You guide the world with kindness, its creatures with compassion. God neither slumbers nor sleeps. You stir the sleeping, support the falling, free the fettered, raise those bowed down and give voice to the speechless. You alone do we acknowledge.

Could song fill our mouth as water fills the sea,
    And could joy flood our tongue like countless waves,
Could our lips utter praise as limitless as sky,
    And could our eyes match the splendor of the sun,
Could we soar with arms like eagle's wings,
    And run with the gentle grace of swiftest deer,
Never could we fully state our gratitude
For one ten-thousandth of the lasting love
    Which is Your precious blessing, dearest God,
    Granted to our ancestors and us.

From Mitzrayim You redeemed us, from the house of bondage You delivered us. In famine You nourished us, in prosperity You sustained us. You rescued us from the sword, protected us from pestilence and saved us from severe and lingering disease. To this day Your compassion has helped us, Your kindness has not forsaken us. Never abandon us, Adonai our God. These limbs which You formed for us, this soul-force which You breathed into us, this tongue which You set in our mouth, must thank, praise, extol, exalt and sing Your holiness and sovereignty. Every mouth shall thank You, every tongue shall pledge

וְכָל בֶּרֶךְ לְךָ תִכְרַע, וְכָל קוֹמָה לְפָנֶיךָ תִשְׁתַּחֲוֶה, וְכָל לְבָבוֹת יִירָאוּךָ, וְכָל קֶרֶב וּכְלָיוֹת יְזַמְּרוּ לִשְׁמֶךָ. כַּדָּבָר שֶׁכָּתוּב: כָּל עַצְמוֹתַי תֹּאמַרְנָה, יהוה מִי כָמוֹךָ, מַצִּיל עָנִי מֵחָזָק מִמֶּנּוּ, וְעָנִי וְאֶבְיוֹן מִגֹּזְלוֹ. מִי יִדְמֶה לָךְ וּמִי יִשְׁוֶה לָךְ וּמִי יַעֲרָךְ לָךְ, הָאֵל הַגָּדוֹל הַגִּבּוֹר וְהַנּוֹרָא, אֵל עֶלְיוֹן, קֹנֵה שָׁמַיִם וָאָרֶץ. נְהַלֶּלְךָ וּנְשַׁבֵּחֲךָ וּנְפָאֶרְךָ וּנְבָרֵךְ אֶת שֵׁם קָדְשֶׁךָ, כָּאָמוּר: לְדָוִד. בָּרְכִי נַפְשִׁי אֶת יהוה, וְכָל קְרָבַי אֶת שֵׁם קָדְשׁוֹ.

הָאֵל בְּתַעֲצֻמוֹת עֻזֶּךָ, הַגָּדוֹל בִּכְבוֹד שְׁמֶךָ, הַגִּבּוֹר לָנֶצַח וְהַנּוֹרָא בְּנוֹרְאוֹתֶיךָ, הַמֶּלֶךְ הַיּוֹשֵׁב עַל כִּסֵּא רָם וְנִשָּׂא.

שׁוֹכֵן עַד, מָרוֹם וְקָדוֹשׁ שְׁמוֹ. וְכָתוּב: רַנְּנוּ צַדִּיקִים בַּיהוה, לַיְשָׁרִים נָאוָה תְהִלָּה. בְּפִי יְשָׁרִים תִּתְהַלָּל וּבְדִבְרֵי צַדִּיקִים תִּתְבָּרַךְ וּבִלְשׁוֹן חֲסִידִים תִּתְרוֹמָם וּבְקֶרֶב קְדוֹשִׁים תִּתְקַדָּשׁ.

וּבְמַקְהֲלוֹת רִבְבוֹת עַמְּךָ בֵּית יִשְׂרָאֵל, בְּרִנָּה יִתְפָּאַר שִׁמְךָ מַלְכֵּנוּ בְּכָל דּוֹר וָדוֹר. שֶׁכֵּן חוֹבַת כָּל הַיְצוּרִים לְפָנֶיךָ, יהוה אֱלֹהֵינוּ וֵאלֹהֵי אֲבוֹתֵינוּ, לְהוֹדוֹת לְהַלֵּל לְשַׁבֵּחַ, לְפָאֵר לְרוֹמֵם לְהַדֵּר, לְבָרֵךְ לְעַלֵּה וּלְקַלֵּס עַל כָּל דִּבְרֵי שִׁירוֹת וְתִשְׁבָּחוֹת דָּוִד בֶּן יִשַׁי עַבְדְּךָ מְשִׁיחֶךָ.

יִשְׁתַּבַּח שִׁמְךָ לָעַד מַלְכֵּנוּ, הָאֵל הַמֶּלֶךְ הַגָּדוֹל וְהַקָּדוֹשׁ בַּשָּׁמַיִם וּבָאָרֶץ. כִּי לְךָ נָאֶה, יהוה אֱלֹהֵינוּ וֵאלֹהֵי אֲבוֹתֵינוּ, שִׁיר וּשְׁבָחָה, הַלֵּל וְזִמְרָה, עֹז וּמֶמְשָׁלָה, נֶצַח, גְּדֻלָּה וּגְבוּרָה, תְּהִלָּה וְתִפְאֶרֶת, קְדֻשָּׁה וּמַלְכוּת, בְּרָכוֹת וְהוֹדָאוֹת מֵעַתָּה וְעַד עוֹלָם. בָּרוּךְ אַתָּה יהוה אֵל מֶלֶךְ גָּדוֹל בַּתִּשְׁבָּחוֹת, אֵל הַהוֹדָאוֹת, אֲדוֹן הַנִּפְלָאוֹת, הַבּוֹחֵר בְּשִׁירֵי זִמְרָה, מֶלֶךְ, אֵל, חֵי הָעוֹלָמִים.

Fifteenfold finale. Fifteen expressions of praise are used in the paragraph that begins, "You shall always be praised," the climax and conclusion of *Nishmat.* Fifteen is a number with numerous liturgical associations. Fifteen "Songs of Ascent" (Psalms 120 to 134) were chanted by the Levites as they ascended the fifteen steps to the Temple. Fifteen words comprise the priestly benediction. Fifteen generations are counted from our founding father Abraham to the builder of the Temple, Solomon. Fifteen is the numerical value of *Yah*, an abbreviated form of the *shem hameforash*, the never-pronounced name of God. Pesaḥ starts on the fifteenth of Nisan. And fifteen signposts, the rubrics from *Kadesh* to *Nirtzah*, guide us through the Seder.

devotion. Every head shall bow to You, every knee shall bend to You, every heart shall revere You, every fiber of our being shall sing Your glory, as the Psalmist sang: "All my bones exclaim—Adonai, who is like You, saving the weak from the powerful, the needy from those who would prey on them?" Who can equal You, who can be compared to You, great, mighty, awesome, exalted God, Creator of heaven and earth? We extol You even as David sang: "Praise Adonai, my soul; let every fiber of my being praise His holy name."

You are God through the vastness of Your power, great through the glory of Your name, mighty forever, awesome through Your awesome works. You are King, enthroned supreme.

He inhabits eternity, sacred and exalted. As the Psalmist has written: Rejoice in Adonai, you righteous. It is fitting for the upright to praise Him.
By the mouth of the upright are You extolled,
by the words of the righteous are You praised,
by the tongue of the faithful are You acclaimed,
in the heart of the saintly are You hallowed.

Among assembled throngs of the House of Israel in every generation Your name shall be glorified in song, our King. For it is the duty of all creatures, Adonai our God and God of our ancestors, to thank, laud and glorify You, extolling, exalting, to add our own praise to the songs of David, Your anointed servant.

You shall always be praised, great and holy God, our King in heaven and on earth. Songs of praise and psalms of gratitude become You, acknowledging Your might and Your dominion. Yours are strength and sovereignty, sanctity, grandeur and glory always. We offer You our devotion, open our hearts in thanksgiving. Praised are You, Sovereign of wonders, crowned with adoration, delighting in mortal song and psalm, exalted King, eternal life of the universe.

כי לו נאה
KI LO NA'EH

כִּי לוֹ נָאֶה. כִּי לוֹ יָאֶה.

For to Him praise is proper, for to Him praise is due.

Ki lo na'eh, ki lo ya'eh.

אַדִּיר בִּמְלוּכָה, בָּחוּר כַּהֲלָכָה, גְּדוּדָיו יֹאמְרוּ לוֹ:
לְךָ וּלְךָ, לְךָ כִּי לְךָ, לְךָ אַף לְךָ, לְךָ יְיָ הַמַּמְלָכָה.
כִּי לוֹ נָאֶה, כִּי לוֹ יָאֶה.

Adir bim-lukhah, baḥur ka-halakhah, gedudav yomru lo.

(REFRAIN)
Lekha u-lekha, lekha ki lekha, lekha af lekha.
Lekha adonai ha-mamlakhah.
Ki lo na'eh, ki lo ya'eh.

דָּגוּל בִּמְלוּכָה, הָדוּר כַּהֲלָכָה, וָתִיקָיו יֹאמְרוּ לוֹ:
לְךָ וּלְךָ, לְךָ כִּי לְךָ, לְךָ אַף לְךָ, לְךָ יְיָ הַמַּמְלָכָה.
כִּי לוֹ נָאֶה, כִּי לוֹ יָאֶה.

Dagul bim-lukhah, hadur ka-halakhah, vatikav yomru lo.
(REFRAIN)

זַכַּאי בִּמְלוּכָה, חָסִין כַּהֲלָכָה, טַפְסָרָיו יֹאמְרוּ לוֹ:
לְךָ וּלְךָ, לְךָ כִּי לְךָ, לְךָ אַף לְךָ, לְךָ יְיָ הַמַּמְלָכָה.
כִּי לוֹ נָאֶה, כִּי לוֹ יָאֶה.

Zakai bim-lukhah, ḥasin ka-halakhah, tafsirav yomru lo.
(REFRAIN)

יָחִיד בִּמְלוּכָה, כַּבִּיר כַּהֲלָכָה, לִמּוּדָיו יֹאמְרוּ לוֹ:
לְךָ וּלְךָ. לְךָ כִּי לְךָ, לְךָ אַף לְךָ, לְךָ יְיָ הַמַּמְלָכָה.
כִּי לוֹ נָאֶה, כִּי לוֹ יָאֶה.

Yahid bim-lukhah, kabir ka-halakhah, limudav yomru lo.
(REFRAIN)

"How can we laud God? Let us count the ways." So the anonymous authors of Ki lo Na'eh and Adir Hu (page 120) may have reasoned. For these hymns run the gamut of the aleph-bet, heaping honorific upon honorific, hosanna upon hosanna. Translations have been omitted since the literal meaning is secondary to the motivation: to praise to the skies the Creator of heaven and earth, the Ancient of Days, our God who is exalted beyond all blessing and praise.

To Him praise is proper. How does one express the inexpressible? The urge to proclaim the glory of God is counterbalanced by the knowledge that such utterances are at worst blasphemous and at best inadequate. Quantitatively, qualitatively, our vocabulary is too limited to do justice to the limitlessness of God. For this reason the Rabbis consider verbal excesses—the multiplication of magniloquent phrases—improper. And therefore "silence is praise." But poets will be poets, and they will not be silenced. Often lyrical liturgists took refuge in alphabetic acrostics, thereby imposing stylistic limitations upon their passion and their poetry.

Prosaic postscript: arranging stanzas alphabetically makes them easier to remember.

מוֹשֵׁל בִּמְלוּכָה, נוֹרָא כַּהֲלָכָה, סְבִיבָיו יֹאמְרוּ לוֹ:
לְךָ וּלְךָ, לְךָ כִּי לְךָ, לְךָ אַף לְךָ, לְךָ יְיָ הַמַּמְלָכָה.
כִּי לוֹ נָאֶה, כִּי לוֹ יָאֶה.

Mosheil bim-lukhah, nora ka-halakhah, sevivav yomru lo.
  (REFRAIN)

עָנָיו בִּמְלוּכָה, פּוֹדֶה כַּהֲלָכָה, צַדִּיקָיו יֹאמְרוּ לוֹ:
לְךָ וּלְךָ, לְךָ כִּי לְךָ, לְךָ אַף לְךָ, לְךָ יְיָ הַמַּמְלָכָה.
כִּי לוֹ נָאֶה, כִּי לוֹ יָאֶה.

Anav bim-lukhah, podeh ka-halakhah, tzadikav yomru lo.
  (REFRAIN)

קָדוֹשׁ בִּמְלוּכָה, רַחוּם כַּהֲלָכָה, שִׁנְאַנָּיו יֹאמְרוּ לוֹ:
לְךָ וּלְךָ, לְךָ כִּי לְךָ, לְךָ אַף לְךָ, לְךָ יְיָ הַמַּמְלָכָה.
כִּי לוֹ נָאֶה, כִּי לוֹ יָאֶה.

Kadosh bim-lukhah, raḥum ka-halakhah, shin-anav yomru lo.
  (REFRAIN)

תַּקִּיף בִּמְלוּכָה, תּוֹמֵךְ כַּהֲלָכָה, תְּמִימָיו יֹאמְרוּ לוֹ:
לְךָ וּלְךָ, לְךָ כִּי לְךָ, לְךָ אַף לְךָ, לְךָ יְיָ הַמַּמְלָכָה.
כִּי לוֹ נָאֶה, כִּי לוֹ יָאֶה.

Takif bim-lukhah, tomeikh ka-halakhah, temimav yomru lo.
  (REFRAIN)

אדיר הוא

ADIR HU
Mighty Is He

אַדִּיר הוּא, יִבְנֶה בֵיתוֹ בְּקָרוֹב, בִּמְהֵרָה בִּמְהֵרָה,
בְּיָמֵינוּ בְּקָרוֹב. אֵל בְּנֵה, אֵל בְּנֵה, בְּנֵה בֵיתְךָ בְּקָרוֹב.

Adir hu, adir hu.

(REFRAIN)

Yivneh veito be-karov,
Bim-hei-rah, bim-hei-rah,
Be-ya-meinu be-karov.
Eil be-nei, Eil be-nei,
Be-nei veit-kha be-karov.

בָּחוּר הוּא, גָּדוֹל הוּא, דָּגוּל הוּא, יִבְנֶה בֵיתוֹ בְּקָרוֹב,
בִּמְהֵרָה בִּמְהֵרָה, בְּיָמֵינוּ בְּקָרוֹב. אֵל בְּנֵה, אֵל בְּנֵה,
בְּנֵה בֵיתְךָ בְּקָרוֹב.

Baḥur hu, gadol hu, dagul hu. (REFRAIN)

הָדוּר הוּא, וָתִיק הוּא, זַכַּאי הוּא, יִבְנֶה בֵיתוֹ בְּקָרוֹב,
בִּמְהֵרָה בִּמְהֵרָה, בְּיָמֵינוּ בְּקָרוֹב. אֵל בְּנֵה, אֵל בְּנֵה,
בְּנֵה בֵיתְךָ בְּקָרוֹב.

Hadur hu, vatik hu, zakai hu. (REFRAIN)

May He rebuild the Temple. In the refrain that pleads for the rebuilding of the *beit hamikdash*, the Temple is the symbol of Israel's restoration — and the inauguration of the messianic age.

The Temple. Geology and theology coalesce in the legend that assigns topographical centrality to the Sanctuary. Thus the construction of the world began with the foundation-stone (*even she-tiyah*) of the Temple, for the Temple is the center of the Holy City, the Holy City is the center of the Holy Land, and the Holy Land is the center of the earth.

Swiftly, in our days. "A thousand years in Your sight are but as yesterday when it is past" (Psalms 90:4). God's ways are not our ways, nor is His time-frame our time-frame. Hence, we plead with a sense of urgency for a quickening of the divine chronometer.

חָסִיד הוּא, טָהוֹר הוּא, יָחִיד הוּא, יִבְנֶה בֵיתוֹ בְּקָרוֹב, בִּמְהֵרָה בִּמְהֵרָה, בְּיָמֵינוּ בְּקָרוֹב. אֵל בְּנֵה, אֵל בְּנֵה, בְּנֵה בֵיתְךָ בְּקָרוֹב.

Ḥasid hu, tahor hu, yaḥid hu. (REFRAIN)

כַּבִּיר הוּא, לָמוּד הוּא, מֶלֶךְ הוּא, יִבְנֶה בֵיתוֹ בְּקָרוֹב, בִּמְהֵרָה בִּמְהֵרָה, בְּיָמֵינוּ בְּקָרוֹב. אֵל בְּנֵה, אֵל בְּנֵה, בְּנֵה בֵיתְךָ בְּקָרוֹב.

Kabir hu, lamud hu, melekh hu. (REFRAIN)

נוֹרָא הוּא, סַגִּיב הוּא, עִזּוּז הוּא, יִבְנֶה בֵיתוֹ בְּקָרוֹב, בִּמְהֵרָה בִּמְהֵרָה, בְּיָמֵינוּ בְּקָרוֹב. אֵל בְּנֵה, אֵל בְּנֵה, בְּנֵה בֵיתְךָ בְּקָרוֹב.

Nora hu, sagiv hu, ee-zuz hu. (REFRAIN)

פּוֹדֶה הוּא, צַדִּיק הוּא, קָדוֹש הוּא, יִבְנֶה בֵיתוֹ בְּקָרוֹב, בִּמְהֵרָה בִּמְהֵרָה, בְּיָמֵינוּ בְּקָרוֹב. אֵל בְּנֵה, אֵל בְּנֵה, בְּנֵה בֵיתְךָ בְּקָרוֹב.

Podeh hu, tzadik hu, kadosh hu. (REFRAIN)

רַחוּם הוּא, שַׁדַּי הוּא, תַּקִּיף הוּא, יִבְנֶה בֵיתוֹ בְּקָרוֹב, בִּמְהֵרָה בִּמְהֵרָה, בְּיָמֵינוּ בְּקָרוֹב. אֵל בְּנֵה, אֵל בְּנֵה, בְּנֵה בֵיתְךָ בְּקָרוֹב.

Raḥum hu, shaddai hu, takif hu. (REFRAIN)

אֶחָד מִי יוֹדֵעַ

אֶחָד מִי יוֹדֵעַ? אֶחָד אֲנִי יוֹדֵעַ: אֶחָד אֱלֹהֵינוּ שֶׁבַּשָּׁמַיִם וּבָאָרֶץ.

שְׁנַיִם מִי יוֹדֵעַ? שְׁנַיִם אֲנִי יוֹדֵעַ: שְׁנֵי לֻחוֹת הַבְּרִית, אֶחָד אֱלֹהֵינוּ שֶׁבַּשָּׁמַיִם וּבָאָרֶץ.

שְׁלֹשָׁה מִי יוֹדֵעַ? שְׁלֹשָׁה אֲנִי יוֹדֵעַ: שְׁלֹשָׁה אָבוֹת, שְׁנֵי לֻחוֹת הַבְּרִית, אֶחָד אֱלֹהֵינוּ שֶׁבַּשָּׁמַיִם וּבָאָרֶץ.

אַרְבַּע מִי יוֹדֵעַ? אַרְבַּע אֲנִי יוֹדֵעַ: אַרְבַּע אִמָּהוֹת, שְׁלֹשָׁה אָבוֹת, שְׁנֵי לֻחוֹת הַבְּרִית, אֶחָד אֱלֹהֵינוּ שֶׁבַּשָּׁמַיִם וּבָאָרֶץ.

חֲמִשָּׁה מִי יוֹדֵעַ? חֲמִשָּׁה אֲנִי יוֹדֵעַ: חֲמִשָּׁה חוּמְשֵׁי תוֹרָה, אַרְבַּע אִמָּהוֹת, שְׁלֹשָׁה אָבוֹת, שְׁנֵי לֻחוֹת הַבְּרִית, אֶחָד אֱלֹהֵינוּ שֶׁבַּשָּׁמַיִם וּבָאָרֶץ.

שִׁשָּׁה מִי יוֹדֵעַ? שִׁשָּׁה אֲנִי יוֹדֵעַ: שִׁשָּׁה סִדְרֵי מִשְׁנָה, חֲמִשָּׁה חוּמְשֵׁי תוֹרָה, אַרְבַּע אִמָּהוֹת, שְׁלֹשָׁה אָבוֹת, שְׁנֵי לֻחוֹת הַבְּרִית, אֶחָד אֱלֹהֵינוּ שֶׁבַּשָּׁמַיִם וּבָאָרֶץ.

שִׁבְעָה מִי יוֹדֵעַ? שִׁבְעָה אֲנִי יוֹדֵעַ: שִׁבְעָה יְמֵי שַׁבְּתָא, שִׁשָּׁה סִדְרֵי מִשְׁנָה, חֲמִשָּׁה חוּמְשֵׁי תוֹרָה, אַרְבַּע אִמָּהוֹת, שְׁלֹשָׁה אָבוֹת, שְׁנֵי לֻחוֹת הַבְּרִית, אֶחָד אֱלֹהֵינוּ שֶׁבַּשָּׁמַיִם וּבָאָרֶץ.

שְׁמוֹנָה מִי יוֹדֵעַ? שְׁמוֹנָה אֲנִי יוֹדֵעַ: שְׁמוֹנָה יְמֵי מִילָה, שִׁבְעָה יְמֵי שַׁבְּתָא, שִׁשָּׁה סִדְרֵי מִשְׁנָה, חֲמִשָּׁה חוּמְשֵׁי תוֹרָה, אַרְבַּע אִמָּהוֹת, שְׁלֹשָׁה אָבוֹת, שְׁנֵי לֻחוֹת הַבְּרִית, אֶחָד אֱלֹהֵינוּ שֶׁבַּשָּׁמַיִם וּבָאָרֶץ.

Who knows? Behind the artless questions contained in this "counting song" lurks the most mystifying question of all. Why was Israel redeemed? The answer spelled out in these verses is that we were redeemed on the basis of the world's first (and probably most unusual) merit system: merits in hand and merits to be earned. The children of the patriarchs, sometimes divided, sometimes divisive, had united to shoulder freely the yoke of the Torah, and through the turbulent centuries they elected to remain true to this commitment, to live for it, even to die for it. A chosen people, as Israel Zangwill once observed, is a choosing people.

Who knows one? The Oneness of God is the sapphire rock upon which our faith is founded. "Hear O Israel . . . Adonai is One" is a simple declaration so fraught with complexity that a seventeenth century mystic, Heshel Tsoref of Vilna, devoted some 5,000 pages to the theosophical and eschatalogical mysteries of this one phrase.

Who knows one? When worshippers declare the unity of the Holy Name in love and reverence (so attests the Zohar), the walls of earth's darkness are cleft in twain and the face of the Heavenly King is revealed, lighting up the universe.

Who knows three? Everything that is closely connected with Israel is triple in number. The Bible consists of three parts, the Torah, the Prophets and the Writings. The communication between God and Israel was carried on by Moses, Aaron and Miriam. The third of Adam's sons, Seth, became the ancestor of humanity, and the third of Noah's sons, Shem, attained high status. Among the Jewish kings, it was the third, Solomon, whom God distinguished above all others.

122

EHAD MI YODEI-A
Who Knows One?

Who knows one?
I know one.

One is our God in heaven and on earth.
Ehad eloheinu sheh-ba-shamayim u-va-aretz.

Who knows two?
I know two.

Two are the tablets of the covenant.
One is our God in heaven and on earth.

Who knows three?
I know three.

Three are the patriarchs.
Two are the tablets of the covenant.
One is our God in heaven and on earth.

Who knows four?
I know four.

Four are the matriarchs.
Three are the patriarchs.
Two are the tablets of the covenant.
One is our God in heaven and on earth.

Who knows five?
I know five.

Five are the books of the Torah.
Four are the matriarchs.
Three are the patriarchs.
Two are the tablets of the covenant.
One is our God in heaven and on earth.

Who knows six?
I know six.

Six are the sections of the Mishnah.
Five are the books of the Torah.
Four are the matriarchs.
Three are the patriarchs.
Two are the tablets of the covenant.
One is our God in heaven and on earth.

Who knows seven?
I know seven.

Seven are the days of the week.
Six are the sections of the Mishnah.
Five are the books of the Torah.
Four are the matriarchs.
Three are the patriarchs.
Two are the tablets of the covenant.
One is our God in heaven and on earth.

Who knows eight?
I know eight.

Eight are the days to circumcision.
Seven are the days of the week.
Six are the sections of the Mishnah.
Five are the books of the Torah.
Four are the matriarchs.
Three are the patriarchs.
Two are the tablets of the covenant.
One is our God in heaven and on earth.

תִּשְׁעָה מִי יוֹדֵעַ? תִּשְׁעָה אֲנִי יוֹדֵעַ: תִּשְׁעָה יַרְחֵי
לֵדָה, שְׁמוֹנָה יְמֵי מִילָה, שִׁבְעָה יְמֵי שַׁבְּתָא, שִׁשָּׁה
סִדְרֵי מִשְׁנָה, חֲמִשָּׁה חוּמְשֵׁי תוֹרָה, אַרְבַּע אִמָּהוֹת,
שְׁלֹשָׁה אָבוֹת, שְׁנֵי לֻחוֹת הַבְּרִית, אֶחָד אֱלֹהֵינוּ
שֶׁבַּשָּׁמַיִם וּבָאָרֶץ.

עֲשָׂרָה מִי יוֹדֵעַ? עֲשָׂרָה אֲנִי יוֹדֵעַ: עֲשָׂרָה דִּבְּרַיָּא,
תִּשְׁעָה יַרְחֵי לֵדָה, שְׁמוֹנָה יְמֵי מִילָה, שִׁבְעָה יְמֵי
שַׁבְּתָא, שִׁשָּׁה סִדְרֵי מִשְׁנָה, חֲמִשָּׁה חוּמְשֵׁי תוֹרָה,
אַרְבַּע אִמָּהוֹת, שְׁלֹשָׁה אָבוֹת, שְׁנֵי לֻחוֹת הַבְּרִית,
אֶחָד אֱלֹהֵינוּ שֶׁבַּשָּׁמַיִם וּבָאָרֶץ.

אַחַד עָשָׂר מִי יוֹדֵעַ? אַחַד עָשָׂר אֲנִי יוֹדֵעַ: אַחַד עָשָׂר
כּוֹכְבַיָּא, עֲשָׂרָה דִּבְּרַיָּא, תִּשְׁעָה יַרְחֵי לֵדָה, שְׁמוֹנָה
יְמֵי מִילָה, שִׁבְעָה יְמֵי שַׁבְּתָא, שִׁשָּׁה סִדְרֵי מִשְׁנָה,
חֲמִשָּׁה חוּמְשֵׁי תוֹרָה, אַרְבַּע אִמָּהוֹת, שְׁלֹשָׁה אָבוֹת,
שְׁנֵי לֻחוֹת הַבְּרִית, אֶחָד אֱלֹהֵינוּ שֶׁבַּשָּׁמַיִם וּבָאָרֶץ.

שְׁנֵים עָשָׂר מִי יוֹדֵעַ? שְׁנֵים עָשָׂר אֲנִי יוֹדֵעַ: שְׁנֵים
עָשָׂר שִׁבְטַיָּא, אַחַד עָשָׂר כּוֹכְבַיָּא, עֲשָׂרָה דִּבְּרַיָּא,
תִּשְׁעָה יַרְחֵי לֵדָה, שְׁמוֹנָה יְמֵי מִילָה, שִׁבְעָה יְמֵי
שַׁבְּתָא, שִׁשָּׁה סִדְרֵי מִשְׁנָה, חֲמִשָּׁה חוּמְשֵׁי תוֹרָה,
אַרְבַּע אִמָּהוֹת, שְׁלֹשָׁה אָבוֹת, שְׁנֵי לֻחוֹת הַבְּרִית,
אֶחָד אֱלֹהֵינוּ שֶׁבַּשָּׁמַיִם וּבָאָרֶץ.

Four are the matriarchs? Sacrificing reason to rhyme, the versifier deals less than fairly with our matriarchs, namely Sarah, Rebekah, Leah, Rachel, Bilhah and Zilpah. However, it is said that the names of all six of Israel's founding mothers (together with the names of the three patriarchs and the twelve tribes) were engraved on the staff of Moses—compensation for this piece of poetic injustice.

Who knows ten? And who knows why there is a tendency for things to happen or appear in tens? With ten words, the world was created. And through ten blows (*makkot*, plagues) the shackles of slavery were riven and Israel was born, a sovereign people.

Who knows twelve? One of the many miracles attending the crossing of the Red Sea is that the waters did not part to leave just one pathway; they formed twelve separate paths, one for each of the tribes. To Rabbi Yehudah Leib Alter of Ger, this signifies that each tribe had a share in the deliverance — so did each member of each tribe and so did every single one of us.

Who knows thirteen? "Adonai, Adonai, merciful and gracious God, slow to anger, abundant in goodness and truth; showing mercy unto the thousandth generation, forgiving iniquity and transgression and sin; but by no means acquitting the impenitent" (Exodus 34:6–7). Thirteen divine attributes are derived from these two verses.

Who knows thirteen? Thirteen is the numerical value of the Hebrew word for ONE (*ehad*) which brings us back full circle to the first stanza of this counting song, the Oneness of God, and to the conclusion that thirteen is a highly auspicious number.

Who knows nine? I know nine.	Nine are the months to childbirth. Eight are the days to circumcision. Seven are the days of the week. Six are the sections of the Mishnah. Five are the books of the Torah. Four are the matriarchs. Three are the patriarchs. Two are the tablets of the covenant. One is our God in heaven and on earth.
Who knows ten? I know ten.	Ten are the commandments at Sinai. Nine are the months to childbirth. Eight are the days to circumcision. Seven are the days of the week. Six are the sections of the Mishnah. Five are the books of the Torah. Four are the matriarchs. Three are the patriarchs. Two are the tablets of the covenant. One is our God in heaven and on earth.
Who knows eleven? I know eleven.	Eleven are the stars of Joseph's dream. Ten are the commandments at Sinai. Nine are the months to childbirth. Eight are the days to circumcision. Seven are the days of the week. Six are the sections of the Mishnah. Five are the books of the Torah. Four are the matriarchs. Three are the patriarchs. Two are the tablets of the covenant. One is our God in heaven and on earth.
Who knows twelve? I know twelve.	Twelve are the tribes of Israel. Eleven are the stars of Joseph's dream. Ten are the commandments at Sinai. Nine are the months to childbirth. Eight are the days to circumcision. Seven are the days of the week. Six are the sections of the Mishnah. Five are the books of the Torah. Four are the matriarchs. Three are the patriarchs. Two are the tablets of the covenant. One is our God in heaven and on earth.

שְׁלֹשָׁה עָשָׂר מִי יוֹדֵעַ?
שְׁלֹשָׁה עָשָׂר אֲנִי יוֹדֵעַ:
שְׁלֹשָׁה עָשָׂר מִדַּיָּא,
שְׁנֵים עָשָׂר שִׁבְטַיָּא,
אַחַד עָשָׂר כּוֹכְבַיָּא,
עֲשָׂרָה דִּבְּרַיָּא,
תִּשְׁעָה יַרְחֵי לֵדָה,
שְׁמוֹנָה יְמֵי מִילָה,
שִׁבְעָה יְמֵי שַׁבְּתָא,
שִׁשָּׁה סִדְרֵי מִשְׁנָה,
חֲמִשָּׁה חוּמְשֵׁי תוֹרָה,
אַרְבַּע אִמָּהוֹת,
שְׁלֹשָׁה אָבוֹת,
שְׁנֵי לֻחוֹת הַבְּרִית,
אֶחָד אֱלֹהֵינוּ
שֶׁבַּשָּׁמַיִם וּבָאָרֶץ.

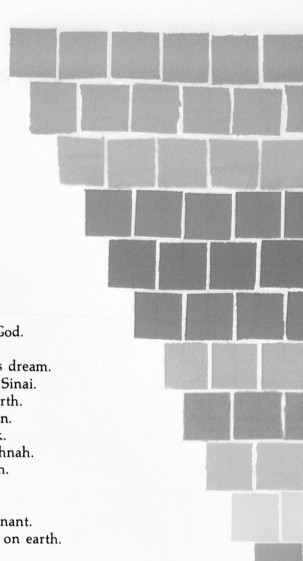

Who knows thirteen?
I know thirteen.

Thirteen are the attributes of God.
Twelve are the tribes of Israel.
Eleven are the stars of Joseph's dream.
Ten are the commandments at Sinai.
Nine are the months to childbirth.
Eight are the days to circumcision.
Seven are the days of the week.
Six are the sections of the Mishnah.
Five are the books of the Torah.
Four are the matriarchs.
Three are the patriarchs.
Two are the tablets of the covenant.
One is our God in heaven and on earth.

חַד גַּדְיָא

חַד גַּדְיָא, חַד גַּדְיָא.
דְּזַבִּן אַבָּא בִּתְרֵי זוּזֵי, חַד גַּדְיָא חַד גַּדְיָא.

וַאֲתָא שׁוּנְרָא וְאָכַל לְגַדְיָא,
דְּזַבִּן אַבָּא בִּתְרֵי זוּזֵי, חַד גַּדְיָא חַד גַּדְיָא.

וַאֲתָא כַלְבָּא וְנָשַׁךְ לְשׁוּנְרָא, דְּאָכַל לְגַדְיָא,
דְּזַבִּן אַבָּא בִּתְרֵי זוּזֵי, חַד גַּדְיָא חַד גַּדְיָא.

וַאֲתָא חוּטְרָא וְהִכָּה לְכַלְבָּא,
דְּנָשַׁךְ לְשׁוּנְרָא, דְּאָכַל לְגַדְיָא,
דְּזַבִּן אַבָּא בִּתְרֵי זוּזֵי, חַד גַּדְיָא חַד גַּדְיָא.

וַאֲתָא נוּרָא וְשָׂרַף לְחוּטְרָא, דְּהִכָּה לְכַלְבָּא,
דְּנָשַׁךְ לְשׁוּנְרָא, דְּאָכַל לְגַדְיָא,
דְּזַבִּן אַבָּא בִּתְרֵי זוּזֵי, חַד גַּדְיָא חַד גַּדְיָא.

וַאֲתָא מַיָּא וְכָבָה לְנוּרָא, דְּשָׂרַף לְחוּטְרָא,
דְּהִכָּה לְכַלְבָּא, דְּנָשַׁךְ לְשׁוּנְרָא, דְּאָכַל לְגַדְיָא,
דְּזַבִּן אַבָּא בִּתְרֵי זוּזֵי, חַד גַּדְיָא חַד גַּדְיָא.

וַאֲתָא תוֹרָא וְשָׁתָה לְמַיָּא, דְּכָבָה לְנוּרָא,
דְּשָׂרַף לְחוּטְרָא, דְּהִכָּה לְכַלְבָּא,
דְּנָשַׁךְ לְשׁוּנְרָא, דְּאָכַל לְגַדְיָא,
דְּזַבִּן אַבָּא בִּתְרֵי זוּזֵי, חַד גַּדְיָא חַד גַּדְיָא.

וַאֲתָא הַשּׁוֹחֵט וְשָׁחַט לְתוֹרָא, דְּשָׁתָה לְמַיָּא,
דְּכָבָה לְנוּרָא, דְּשָׂרַף לְחוּטְרָא, דְּהִכָּה לְכַלְבָּא,
דְּנָשַׁךְ לְשׁוּנְרָא, דְּאָכַל לְגַדְיָא,
דְּזַבִּן אַבָּא בִּתְרֵי זוּזֵי, חַד גַּדְיָא חַד גַּדְיָא.

Is this singable ditty a simplistic nursery rhyme version of cause and effect, crime and punishment? Or is it an allegory of Israel's fate among the nations? In the light of the second theory, the one-of-a-kind kid is Israel, purchased by the Almighty for two zuzim (the two tablets of the Torah or Moses and Aaron). And here is the cast of Israel's oppressors, identified in order of appearance (or disappearance) as: Assyria (the cat), Babylon (the dog), Persia (the stick), Greece (the fire), Rome (the water), the Saracens (the ox), the Crusaders (the shoḥet), the Ottomans (the angel of death). But all's well that ends well. For, "If you see the oppression of the poor and the violent perverting of justice and righteousness in the state, marvel not at the matter; for one higher than the high watches" (Ecclesiastes 5:7). As the curtain comes down on this miniature morality play, retribution is exacted and death dies, confounded forever. So the Seder ends on a note of jubilation and the prospect of life everlasting.

128

ḤAD GADYA

One Kid, Just One Kid

One kid, just one kid.
My father bought for two zuzim, one kid, just one kid.

Then came a cat and ate the kid
that my father bought for two zuzim,
had gadya, had gadya.

Then came a dog and bit the cat
  that ate the kid
that my father bought for two zuzim,
had gadya, had gadya.

Then came a stick and beat the dog
  that bit the cat that ate the kid
that my father bought for two zuzim,
had gadya, had gadya.

Then came a fire and burnt the stick
  that beat the dog that bit the cat that ate the kid
that my father bought for two zuzim,
had gadya, had gadya.

Then came water and quenched the fire
  that burnt the stick that beat the dog
  that bit the cat that ate the kid
that my father bought for two zuzim,
had gadya, had gadya.

Then came an ox and drank the water
  that quenched the fire that burnt the stick
  that beat the dog that bit the cat that ate the kid
that my father bought for two zuzim,
had gadya, had gadya.

Then came a shoḥet and slaughtered the ox
  that drank the water that quenched the fire
  that burnt the stick that beat the dog
  that bit the cat that ate the kid
that my father bought for two zuzim,
had gadya, had gadya,

וַאֲתָא מַלְאַךְ הַמָּוֶת וְשָׁחַט לְשׁוֹחֵט, דְּשָׁחַט לְתוֹרָא, דְּשָׁתָה לְמַיָּא, דְּכָבָה לְנוּרָא, דְּשָׂרַף לְחוּטְרָא, דְּהִכָּה לְכַלְבָּא, דְּנָשַׁךְ לְשׁוּנְרָא, דְּאָכַל לְגַדְיָא, דְּזַבֵּן אַבָּא בִּתְרֵי זוּזֵי, חַד גַּדְיָא חַד גַּדְיָא.

וַאֲתָא הַקָּדוֹשׁ בָּרוּךְ הוּא וְשָׁחַט לְמַלְאַךְ הַמָּוֶת, דְּשָׁחַט לְשׁוֹחֵט, דְּשָׁחַט לְתוֹרָא, דְּשָׁתָה לְמַיָּא, דְּכָבָה לְנוּרָא, דְּשָׂרַף לְחוּטְרָא, דְּהִכָּה לְכַלְבָּא, דְּנָשַׁךְ לְשׁוּנְרָא, דְּאָכַל לְגַדְיָא, דְּזַבֵּן אַבָּא בִּתְרֵי זוּזֵי, חַד גַּדְיָא חַד גַּדְיָא.

Just one Kid. One hundred and thirty years after Jacob had settled in Mitzrayim, Pharaoh dreamed a dream that filled him with dread. In his dream he saw a balance. On one scale were the mighty men of Mitzrayim, bound together. On the other scale lay a young kid. And the tender kid outweighed all of Mitzrayim. Then Pharaoh took counsel with the wisest of his wise men. What did the dream portend? That a child would be born in Israel who would wreak havoc in Mitzrayim in order to lead his folk to freedom. What should be done? Pleaded Jethro: "Let this people go to the land of their ancestors." Countered Balaam: "Let their name be wiped off the face of the earth. Cast every newborn Hebrew male into the Nile." Balaam's preachments prevailed. Jethro, banished to Midian, became the father-in-law of Moses. Balaam learned a humiliating lesson from the donkey's mouth. And Pharaoh found out that a power-mad potentate, dressed in a little brief authority, was powerless to circumvent God's plan for the liberation of man from human bondage.

Then came the angel of death who killed the shoḥet
   who slaughtered the ox that drank the water
   that quenched the fire that burnt the stick
   that beat the dog that bit the cat that ate the kid
that my father bought for two zuzim,
ḥad gadya, ḥad gadya.

Then came the Holy One and killed the angel of death
   who killed the shoḥet
   who slaughtered the ox
   that drank the water
   that quenched the fire
   that burnt the stick
   that beat the dog
   that bit the cat
   that ate the kid
that my father bought for two zuzim,
ḥad gadya, ḥad gadya.

ספירת העומר

Rise and recite:

בָּרוּךְ אַתָּה יהוה אֱלֹהֵינוּ מֶלֶךְ הָעוֹלָם אֲשֶׁר קִדְּשָׁנוּ בְּמִצְוֹתָיו וְצִוָּנוּ עַל סְפִירַת הָעֹמֶר.

הַיּוֹם יוֹם אֶחָד לָעֹמֶר.

Reflection:

רִבּוֹנוֹ שֶׁל עוֹלָם, אַתָּה צִוִּיתָנוּ עַל יְדֵי מֹשֶׁה עַבְדְּךָ לִסְפּוֹר סְפִירַת הָעֹמֶר, כְּמוֹ שֶׁכָּתַבְתָּ בְּתוֹרָתֶךָ: וּסְפַרְתֶּם לָכֶם מִמָּחֳרַת הַשַּׁבָּת מִיּוֹם הֲבִיאֲכֶם אֶת עֹמֶר הַתְּנוּפָה שֶׁבַע שַׁבָּתוֹת תְּמִימוֹת תִּהְיֶינָה. עַד מִמָּחֳרַת הַשַּׁבָּת הַשְּׁבִיעִית תִּסְפְּרוּ חֲמִשִּׁים יוֹם. וּבְכֵן יְהִי רָצוֹן מִלְּפָנֶיךָ יהוה אֱלֹהֵינוּ וֵאלֹהֵי אֲבוֹתֵינוּ שֶׁבִּזְכוּת סְפִירַת הָעֹמֶר שֶׁסָּפַרְתִּי הַיּוֹם יְתַקַּן מַה שֶּׁפָּגַמְתִּי בִּסְפִירָה, וְאֶטָּהֵר וְאֶתְקַדֵּשׁ בִּקְדֻשָּׁה שֶׁל מַעְלָה, אָמֵן סֶלָה.

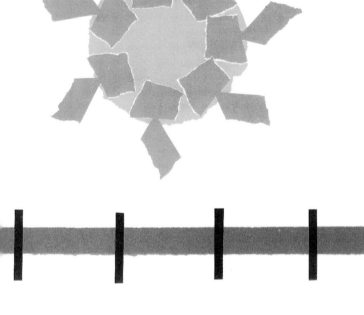

HOW: Every evening, from the second night of Pesaḥ until the night before Shavuot, we count the days of the *Omer.*

WHY: *Omer* (literally "sheaf") refers to the offering from the new barley crop which was brought to the Temple on the sixteenth of Nisan, the eve of the second day of Pesaḥ. *Omer* has come to be the name of the period between Pesaḥ and Shavuot. By counting the days of this period (*sefirat ha-omer*), we recall the events which they connect, the liberation from enslavement commemorated by Pesaḥ and the gift of Revelation commemorated by Shavuot, events which took place during our people's journey to the Promised Land. On our personal journeys in life we each have our own enslavements and liberations, revelations and promised lands. As we often count the days leading to significant events in our personal lives, so we count such days in the life of our people, times past and present. We also recall that our ancestors were closely connected with the soil, directly dependent upon crops, and we recount their gratitude for the harvest of grain through which God renews life each year.

Counting the Omer

(recited only on the second night)

Counting the Omer. Why do we literally check off the days between Pesaḥ and Shavuot? "Just as one who expects his dearest friend on a certain day counts the days and even the hours ... we count the days that follow the offering of the *Omer*, between the anniversary of our departure from Mitzrayim and the anniversary of our arrival at Sinai and the Giving of the Torah." The number forty-nine can also be associated with the forty-nine gates of purity through which Israel graduated, by God's grace, passing day after day through gate after gate, as God brought His people closer and closer to Sinai and Himself.

Rise and recite:

Praised are You, Adonai our God, King of the universe whose *mitzvot* add holiness to our lives and who gave us the *mitzvah* of counting the *Omer*.

Today is the first day of the *Omer*.

Reflection:

Master of the universe, You commanded us to count the *Omer*, as You have written in Your Torah: "From the eve of the second day of Pesaḥ, when an *Omer* of grain is to be brought as an offering, you shall count seven complete weeks. The day after the seventh week of your counting will make fifty days" (Leviticus 23:15–16). Adonai our God and God of our ancestors, may it be counted in my favor that I have dutifully counted the *Omer* today, and may I thereby make amends for any harm that I may have done, and may I be purified and sanctified in the holiness of heaven. Amen.

כּוֹס רְבִיעִי

Reflection:

הִנְנִי מוּכָן/מוּכָנָה וּמְזֻמָּן/וּמְזֻמֶּנֶת לְקַיֵּם מִצְוַת כּוֹס רְבִיעִי שֶׁהוּא כְּנֶגֶד בְּשׂוֹרַת הַיְשׁוּעָה שֶׁאָמַר הַקָּדוֹשׁ בָּרוּךְ הוּא לְיִשְׂרָאֵל: וְלָקַחְתִּי אֶתְכֶם לִי לְעָם וְהָיִיתִי לָכֶם לֵאלֹהִים.

Lift the cup of wine and recite:

בָּרוּךְ אַתָּה יהוה אֱלֹהֵינוּ מֶלֶךְ הָעוֹלָם בּוֹרֵא פְּרִי הַגָּפֶן.

Drink the wine while reclining, then recite the following blessing, adding the words in parentheses on Shabbat.

בָּרוּךְ אַתָּה יהוה אֱלֹהֵינוּ מֶלֶךְ הָעוֹלָם עַל הַגֶּפֶן וְעַל פְּרִי הַגֶּפֶן, וְעַל תְּנוּבַת הַשָּׂדֶה וְעַל אֶרֶץ חֶמְדָּה טוֹבָה וּרְחָבָה, שֶׁרָצִיתָ וְהִנְחַלְתָּ לַאֲבוֹתֵינוּ לֶאֱכֹל מִפִּרְיָהּ וְלִשְׂבּוֹעַ מִטּוּבָהּ. רַחֶם נָא יהוה אֱלֹהֵינוּ עַל יִשְׂרָאֵל עַמֶּךְ וְעַל יְרוּשָׁלַיִם עִירֶךָ, וְעַל צִיּוֹן מִשְׁכַּן כְּבוֹדֶךָ וְעַל מִזְבְּחֶךָ וְעַל הֵיכָלֶךָ. וּבְנֵה יְרוּשָׁלַיִם עִיר הַקֹּדֶשׁ בִּמְהֵרָה בְיָמֵינוּ, וְהַעֲלֵנוּ לְתוֹכָהּ וְשַׂמְּחֵנוּ בְּבִנְיָנָהּ, וְנֹאכַל מִפִּרְיָהּ וְנִשְׂבַּע מִטּוּבָהּ וּנְבָרֶכְךָ עָלֶיהָ בִּקְדֻשָּׁה וּבְטָהֳרָה. (וּרְצֵה וְהַחֲלִיצֵנוּ בְּיוֹם הַשַּׁבָּת הַזֶּה) וְשַׂמְּחֵנוּ בְּיוֹם חַג הַמַּצּוֹת הַזֶּה, כִּי אַתָּה יהוה טוֹב וּמֵטִיב לַכֹּל, וְנוֹדֶה לְּךָ עַל הָאָרֶץ וְעַל פְּרִי הַגָּפֶן. בָּרוּךְ אַתָּה יהוה עַל הָאָרֶץ וְעַל פְּרִי הַגָּפֶן.

Nirtzah

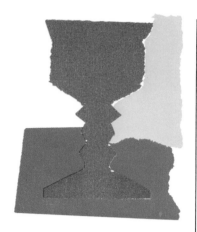

The Fourth Cup

The fruit of the vine. "You plucked a vine out of Mitzrayim . . . and You planted it, and You cleared a place for it, so that it took deep root and filled the land" (Psalms 80:9–10). "A vineyard of Adonai is the house of Israel, and the people of Judah is the plant that delights Him" (Isaiah 5:7). Israel, in the biblical and rabbinic idiom, is often likened to the vine, and this viticultural simile is strangely apposite. Like the fruit of the vine, the Jewish people is crushed repeatedly, yet this agonizing process is the beginning not the end of the story. In the crushing, the fruit of the vine undergoes a startling metamorphosis, turning into heady juices that gladden the heart, mellow and mature with time, becoming the valued companions of connoisseurs. Like the fruit of the vine, Israel is destined for the table of the King of kings.

Reflection:

I am ready to fulfill the commandment of drinking the fourth of the Four Cups. This recalls God's promise of redemption to the people Israel, as it says, "I will take you to be My people and I will be your God" (Exodus 6:7).

Lift the cup of wine and recite:

Praised are You, Adonai our God, King of the universe who creates the fruit of the vine.

Drink the wine while reclining, then recite the following blessing, adding the words in parentheses on Shabbat:

Praised are You, Adonai our God, King of the universe, for the vine and for its fruit. We thank You for the earth's bounty and the pleasing, spacious, desirable land which You gave our ancestors, that they might eat of its produce and be satisfied with its goodly yield. Adonai our God, have mercy on Jerusalem Your city, on Zion the home of Your glory, and on the Temple. Fully restore Jerusalem soon and in our day, so that we may rejoice in its restoration and eat of the land's good fruit in abundance and praise You in holiness. (Renew us this Shabbat.) Grant us joy this Pesah. We thank You, Adonai, for Your goodness to all. We thank You for the land and for the fruit of the vine. Praised are You, Adonai, for the land and for the fruit of the vine.

חֲסַל סִדּוּר פֶּסַח כְּהִלְכָתוֹ,
כְּכָל מִשְׁפָּטוֹ וְחֻקָּתוֹ.
כַּאֲשֶׁר זָכִינוּ לְסַדֵּר אוֹתוֹ,
כֵּן נִזְכֶּה לַעֲשׂוֹתוֹ.
זָךְ שׁוֹכֵן מְעוֹנָה,
קוֹמֵם קְהַל עֲדַת מִי מָנָה.
בְּקָרוֹב נַהֵל נִטְעֵי כַנָּה,
פְּדוּיִם לְצִיּוֹן בְּרִנָּה.

לְשָׁנָה הַבָּאָה בִּירוּשָׁלָיִם.

Hark! my beloved!
Behold, he comes,
Leaping upon the mountains,
Skipping upon the hills.
My beloved is like a gazelle
   or a young hart.
My beloved spoke,
   and said to me:
   "Rise up, my love, my fair one,
   and come away.
For now the winter is past,
The rain is over and gone;
The flowers appear on the earth;
The time of singing has come,
And the voice of the turtle
   is heard in our land;
The fig-tree puts forth
   her green figs,
And the vines in blossom
   give forth their fragrance.
Arise, my love, my fair one,
   and come away"
(Song of Songs 2:8–13).

WHY do we read the Song of Songs (*shir hashirim*) on Pesaḥ? Coinciding with springtime, the earth's annual reawakening from its wintry slumbers, Pesaḥ celebrates Israel's reawakening from its woeful winter of enslavement. *Shir hashirim* sings of spring, of flowering pomegranates and budding vines. It sings of love, a love that cannot be quenched, a love that is sweeter than wine and stronger than death. According to traditionalists, this is the eternal love between Israel and its Redeemer who came "leaping upon the mountains," leaping over space and time to hasten the liberation of His beloved people.

Our Seder now has ended
with its history-laden rites.
We have journeyed from Mitzrayim
on this storied night of nights.
We bore witness, we remembered
our covenant with You.
So we pray that You redeem us
as You pledged Your word to do.

NEXT YEAR IN JERUSALEM!

La-shanah haba'ah birushalayim.

NOTES AND GLOSSARY

ABBAYE, Naḥmani ben Kaylil, 278–338 CE: Babylonian amora (see below), outstanding dialectician, head of the Pumbedita Academy (333–338). His discussions with Rabbah (q.v.) are frequently cited in the Talmud.

AGGADAH (literally, narration): Homiletical, imaginative, allegorical interpretations of Scripture; those sections of rabbinic literature which are not concerned with *halakhah* (q.v.).

AKIVA ben Joseph, c. 40 to 135 CE: Tanna (q.v.), the foremost scholar of his time and one of the most charismatic personalities of all time. Politician and patriot, he rallied to the support of Bar Kokhba. When Rome forbade study of the Torah, he continued to teach it in public, and for this act of "civil disobedience" the Romans executed him.

AMALEKITES: Unprovoked, these predatory nomads waylaid the Israelites in the desert, attacking from the rear, slaughtering the enfeebled, defenseless stragglers (Exodus 17:8–16 and Deuteronomy 25:17–19). Amalek became a byword for wanton militarism, for man's inhumanity to man, for "not fearing God."

AMORA, pl. AMORAIM (literally, lecturers): Interpreters of and commentators on the Mishnah, they flourished between 200 and 500 CE. Their thoughts and teachings comprise the Gemara.

AVOT or PIRKE AVOT (The Fathers, Ethics of the Fathers): One of the sixty-three tractates of the Mishnah, a compendium of the aphorisms of scores of sages who taught from the 3rd century BCE to the 3rd century CE.

BAR KOKHBA, "Son of a Star," Shimon ben Kosiba: The general, hailed by Rabbi Akiva as "the king-messiah," who led a valiant but doomed rebellion against the Romans 133–135 CE, ending catastrophically with nearly 600,000 Jewish casualities and the devastation of Judea.

BEN ZOMA, Shimon, early 2nd century CE: Brilliant tanna who immersed himself in mind-bending mystical studies.

BLOOD LIBEL (*alilat dam*): In the Middle Ages the allegation that Jews use Christian blood in Pesaḥ rituals was used to incite an ignorant peasantry to anti-Jewish excesses. Refuted by many popes, it was promulgated all too effectively by the lesser clergy, and has persisted through the centuries. Revived in postwar Poland, it climaxed in the murder of over 60 Jews in the city of Kielce on July 4, 1946.

BONFILS, Joseph ben Samuel (Tov Elem), 11th century: French scholar-poet, author of the concluding stanzas (page 136) of a liturgical poem describing the laws of Pesaḥ, composed for reading in the synagogue on the Shabbat before Pesaḥ.

BOOK OF THE DEAD: Egyptian funerary texts.

ELAZAR BEN AZARIAH, 1st to 2nd century CE: Statesman-scholar of illustrious lineage, a direct descendant of Ezra the Scribe. Said to have been elected leader of the Academy at the age of eighteen.

ELIEZER BEN HYRCANUS, 1st to 2nd century CE: Renowned tanna, a pupil of Rabbi Yoḥanan ben Zakkai and a teacher of Rabbi Akiva. Established his own Academy at Lydda.

ENOCH: Father of Methuselah, Enoch (Genesis 5:18–24) was one of the saintly figures of the generation before the Flood. He became a popular figure in Jewish mysticism.

GALUT (dispersion): Exile, both physical and spiritual.

GAMLIEL: Several distinguished Rabbis bear this name. The Rabban Gamliel of the Haggadah is variously identified as Gamliel the Elder, president of the Sanhedrin in Jerusalem before the destruction of the Temple, or his grandson, Gamliel II, president of the Sanhedrin in Yavneh, circa 80, after the destruction of the Temple.

GEMARA (completion): Commentary on and supplement to the Mishnah. Together, Mishnah and Gemara make up the Talmud.

HALAKHAH (literally, the way, specifically Jewish law): Rabbinic interpretation of Jewish law. Civil and religious legislation that governs every aspect of life.

ḤAMETZ: Leaven and leaven products proscribed on Pesaḥ.

HILLEL, 1st century BCE: President of the Sanhedrin, "one of the greatest personalities in the annals of Judaism and indeed of all mankind" (L. Finkelstein). While the teachings of the School of Hillel were often hotly disputed by the opposing School of Shammai, the rulings of the former generally prevailed.

JOSEPHUS, Flavius or Joseph ben Mattityahu ha-Cohen, c. 38 to 100 CE: Jewish general who defected to the Romans and who wrote incisive, if slanted, accounts of Jewish life in the first centuries BCE and CE. His works include *The Wars of the Jews* and *Antiquities of the Jews.*

JOSHUA BEN ḤANANIAH, 1st to 2nd century CE: Palestinian tanna, a Levite who had served in the Temple, this sage, like many of his colleagues, earned his living by manual labor. He was a maker of needles.

JUDAH HA-NASI, c. 135 to 220 CE: Patriarch of Judea, final redactor of the Mishnah. A scholar of great repute, Judah the Prince is often called simply "Rabbi."

LABAN: Brother of Rebekah, uncle of Jacob, father of Rachel and Leah.

LURIA, Isaac ben Solomon Ashkenazi, the "Ari" or the Holy Lion, 1534–1572: highly influential kabbalist who lived in Safed.

MAGGID (TELLING, EXPOSITION): Focus of the Pesaḥ Haggadah, the section which recounts the story of the Exodus and God's miraculous deliverance of the Israelites.

MAOT ḤITTIN (literally, money for wheat): Special charity fund set up to ensure that all Jews have ample provisions, including wine, for the festive celebration of Pesaḥ. In talmudic times, compulsory taxes were levied on the community to finance this important fund.

MEKHILTA OF RABBI ISHMAEL: Tannaitic (pre-200 CE) exegetical work on the Book of Exodus.

MIDRASH (to expound, to interpret): Creative talmudic and post-talmudic exegesis of biblical texts intended to uncover new strata of meaning and to elicit new homiletical insights.

MISHNAH (repetition): "The official textbook of the Oral Law," according to Solomon Schechter, the Mishnah is a compilation of Jewish civil and religious laws, as formulated between the years 200 BCE and 200 CE, and edited by Rabbi Judah Ha-Nasi.

MOSES BEN MAIMON (Maimonides), 1135–1204: Philosopher, rationalist, authoritative codifier of Halakhah. Major works: *Mishneh Torah, Guide for the Perplexed.*

NISAN: The month of spring, Nisan is the first month of the Jewish religious year and the seventh month of the civil calendar. Pesaḥ begins on the fifteenth of Nisan.

PESAḤIM (literally, pascal lambs): The tractate of the Talmud which details and discusses the ordinances relating to the observance of Pesaḥ.

PHILO JUDAEUS: Jewish Hellenistic philosopher of the first century CE:

RABBAH, bar Naḥmani, c. 270–330 CE: Babylonian amora, head of the Academy of Pumbedita 309–330 CE.

RASHI, Solomon ben Isaac, 1040–1105: Born at Troyes, France, commentator par excellence on the Bible and the Talmud.

RAV, Abba Arikha, Abba the Tall, early third century CE: Amora, founder and head of the Academy of Sura in Babylonia, an institution with 1,200 students. He and his colleague Samuel figure prominently in the Talmud.

ROSH ḤODESH: The beginning of a new month was regarded as a minor festival by the ancients (and as a minor new year by the mystics), a time for special offerings and special prayers. We still recite special prayers on Rosh Ḥodesh.

SAMUEL, c. 177–257 CE: Babylonian amora, head of the Academy of Nehardea, the "judge of the diaspora" was familiar with Greek, Latin, medicine and astronomy.

SANHEDRIN: Supreme Court of ancient Israel.

SH'KHINAH (dwelling): The numinous presence of God, infusing the world with His glory and accompanying the Jewish people throughout its long night of exile.

TALMUD (teaching); Monumental compilation of early rabbinic wisdom, comprising Mishnah and Gemara. The Palestinian Talmud (Yerushalmi) was compiled by the late 4th century; the Babylonian Talmud (Bavli), a work of 5,894 folio pages and 2,500,000 words, was completed a century later.

TAMARES, Aaron Samuel, 1869–1931: Rabbi of Grodno, Belorussia, a preacher of pacifism.

TANNA, pl. TANNAIM (literally, teachers): scholars of the first two centuries whose legislation and precepts are recorded in the Mishnah.

TARFON, late 1st century: Prominent tanna, colleague (and onetime teacher) of Rabbi Akiva, noted for his wisdom, wit and humility.

TISHA B'AV (Ninth of Av): Fastday commemorating the destruction of both the First Temple (586 BCE) and the Second Temple (70 CE). It is also the anniversary of other national tragedies, among them the fall of the last stronghold against Rome in 135 CE, the expulsion from Spain in 1492, and the birth of Shabbetai Tzvi in 1626.

YAVNEH: Ancient Palestinian city, south of Jaffa. Here, after the destruction of the Second Temple, Rabbi Yoḥanan ben Zakkai established an academy and re-established the Sanhedrin, building a thriving center of scholarship that ensured the survival of Judaism and the continuity of Jewish tradition.

YOM HA'ATZMAUT: Israel Independence Day, commemorating the signing of the Declaration of Independence on May 14, 1948 (Iyar 5, 5708). Hallel and other special prayers and readings are added to the service on this day.

ZOHAR (brightness): The "bible" of the kabbalists, a mystical commentary on the Torah, attributed by some to thirteenth century Spanish scholar Moses de Leon and by others to second century sage Rabbi Shimon bar Yoḥai.

SOURCES

Since "telling a thing in the name of the person who said it brings deliverance to the world" (*Avot* 6:6), diligent efforts have been made to attribute all citations accurately. The editor is responsible for adaptations and unattributed material.

Page 13:	*God and grammar* . . .	adapted from *The Rabbinic Mind* by Rabbi Max Kadushin
Page 15:	*Removing the ḥametz* . . .	from *The Hasidic Anthology* by Rabbi Louis I. Newman
Page 17:	*Reflection* . . .	adapted from the prayer book of Rabbi Isaac Luria
Page 19:	*The people wear white* . . .	*Talmud Yerushalmi, Rosh Hashanah* 1:3
Page 19:	*It has been suggested* . . .	adapted from "The Passover Seder: On Entering the Order of History" by Rabbi Monford Harris, *Judaism* 25:2, Spring 1976
Page 24:	*Sanctifying the seventh day* . . .	from *The Sabbath* by Dr. Abraham Joshua Heschel
Page 24:	*Shabbat and Shapatu* . . .	adapted from *You Shall Be as Gods* by Dr. Erich Fromm
Page 25:	*I am ready* . . .	Rabbi Judah Loew ben Bezalel, Maharal of Prague
Page 25:	*You have chosen us* . . .	from *Understanding Conservative Judaism* by Rabbi Robert Gordis
Page 26:	*Fire* . . .	*Midrash Tehillim* 92:4
Page 26:	*Differentiating* . . .	adapted from *The Origin and Meaning of Hasidism* by Professor Martin Buber
Page 27:	*You hallowed Your people* . . .	from *The Earth is the Lord's* by Dr. Abraham Joshua Heschel
Page 27:	*Adonai differentiates* . . .	*Mishnah Sanhedrin* 4:5
Page 28:	*Unleavened bread is the leveler* . . .	adapted from *Passover Haggadah* by Rabbi Marcus Lehmann
Page 33:	*Says Rabbi Wolfe of Zhitomir* . . .	from *A Beggar in Jerusalem* by Professor Elie Wiesel
Page 33:	*The forty-nine questions* . . .	from *Souls on Fire* by Professor Elie Wiesel
Page 34:	*We were slaves* . . .	adapted from Rabbi Michael Graetz
Page 38:	*Where I wander* . . .	Rabbi Levi Yitzḥak of Berditchev, from *Tales of the Hasidim: Early Masters* by Professor Martin Buber
Page 39:	*The four children* . . .	from "Sons and Mystics" by Rabbi Louis Jacobs
Page 39:	*The child who does not know* . . .	adapted from "Sons and Mystics" by Rabbi Louis Jacobs
Page 42:	*In the beginning* . . .	based upon "The Origin of the Hallel" by Rabbi Louis Finkelstein, *Hebrew Union College Annual* volume 23, part 2, 1950–51
Page 42:	*Our ancestors served idols* . . .	adapted from Rabbi Michael Graetz
Page 43:	*We base our belief* . . .	from *Emunot v'Deot*, chapter 8, by Rav Saadia Gaon
Page 43:	*Four hundred years* . . .	based upon *Yalkut Shimoni, Genesis* 77
Page 44:	*The full meaning* . . .	from *God in Search of Man* by Dr. Abraham Joshua Heschel
Page 45:	*My father was a wandering Aramean*	*Haggadah Shel Pesaḥ*
Page 45:	*With just a few people* . . .	*Haggadah Shel Pesaḥ; Sifrei Devarim* 301
Page 47:	*And sojourned there* . . .	*Haggadah Shel Pesaḥ: Sifrei Devarim* 301
Page 47:	*And there he became a great nation* . . .	*Midrash Hagadol*, Deuteronomy 26:5; *Mekhilta D'rabbi Yishmael, Bo* 5; *Sifrei Devarim* 36
Page 47:	*Mighty and numerous* . . .	*Midrash Hagadol*, Deuteronomy 26:5 *Haggadah Shel Pesaḥ*
Page 47:	*The Egyptians dealt harshly with us* . . .	based upon *Midrash Hagadol*, Exodus 1:8; *Mishnat Rabbi Eliezer*, chapter 17; Rashi to Exodus 1:8
Page 47:	*Another interpretation* . . .	*Midrash Hagadol*, as cited by Rabbi Abraham Isaac Kook in his *Haggadah Shel Pesaḥ*
Page 47:	*Too many for us* . . .	based upon *Sefer Hayashar, Shemot* 112b;125a-b
Page 48:	*When we compare* . . .	from *Pentateuch and Haftorahs* by Dr. J. H. Hertz
Page 49:	*And oppressed us* . . .	*Haggadah Shel Pesaḥ*
Page 49:	*And they imposed hard labor* . . .	based upon *Midrash Hagadol*, Exodus 1:13; *Exodus Rabbah* 1:13

Page 49:   We cried out . . .   *Midrash Hagadol*, Deuteronomy 26:7; *Haggadah Shel Pesaḥ*

Page 49:   The God of our ancestors . . .   based upon *Exodus Rabbah* 1:34
Page 49:   And Adonai heard our plea . . .   based upon *Exodus Rabbah* 2:5
Page 49:   And saw . . .   *Sefer Siftei Kohen*
Page 50:   Miriam remonstrated . . .   *Sotah* 12a
Page 51:   Our affliction . . .   *Midrash Hagadol*, Deuteronomy 26:7; *Yalkut Shimoni* 163; *Sotah* 11b; *Haggadah Shel Pesaḥ*

Page 51:   Our misery . . .   *Midrash Hagadol*, Deuteronomy 26:7; based upon *Seder Eliahu Rabbah* 21; *Haggadah Shel Pesaḥ*

Page 51:   And our oppression . . .   based upon *Yalkut Shimoni* 163; *Exodus Rabbah* 5:20

Page 54:   The redemption from Mitzrayim . . .   Rabbi Abraham Isaac Kook, as quoted in *The Zionist Idea* by Rabbi Arthur Hertzberg

Page 54:   You shall know . . .   Rabbi Aaron Samuel Tamares, translated by Rabbi Everett Gendler, *Judaism* 17:2, Spring 1968

Page 55:   Then Adonai took us . . .   *Haggadah Shel Pesaḥ*; *Midrash Hagadol*, Deuteronomy 26:8

Page 55:   With a mighty hand . . .   based upon *Aggadat Tefillat Shmoneh Esreh*, as cited in *Torah Shleimah* to Exodus 6:6; see *Shibolei Haleket, Inyan Tefillah* 18

Page 55:   With awesome power . . .   *Haggadah Shel Pesaḥ*; *Midrash Hagadol*, Deuteronomy 26:8

Page 55:   With signs . . .   *Haggadah Shel Pesaḥ*
Page 57:   And with wonders . . .   *Midrash Hagadol*, Deuteronomy 26:8, *Midrash Tannaim*

Page 58:   When the waters of the Sea . . .   *Sanhedrin* 39b
Page 58:   The contest . . .   from *Pentateuch and Haftorahs* by Dr. J. H. Hertz
Page 60:   He divided the sea for us . . .   adapted from *Hebrew Myths* by Robert Graves and Dr. Raphael Patai

Page 60:   He led us across . . .   adapted from *Legends of the Jews* by Professor Louis Ginzberg

Page 61:   He took care of us in the desert . . . based upon *Moreh Nevukhim* 3:24 by Moses Maimonides

Page 61:   He gave us the Torah . . .   adapted from *The Kabbalah and Its Symbolism* by Professor Gershom G. Scholem

Page 62:   Psalm 136 praises God . . .   *Genesis Rabbah* 20:9
Page 62:   Not a single one remained . . .   adapted from *Legends of the Jews* by Professor Louis Ginzberg

Page 63:   The miracle . . .   from *Amid These Storms* by Sir Winston Churchill

Page 67:   In each generation . . .   from *Festivals of the Jewish Year* by Dr. Theodore H. Gaster

Page 68:   When the Israeli victory . . .   from *American Judaism* by Rabbi Jacob Neusner
Page 68:   From enslavement to redemption . . .   from *The Meaning of God in Modern Jewish Religion* by Rabbi Mordecai M. Kaplan

Page 68:   From darkness to light . . .   from *Festivals of the Jewish Year* by Theodore H. Gaster

Page 69:   From slavery to freedom . . .   from *Wanderings* by Rabbi Chaim Potok
Page 69:   Sing praises . . .   Rabbi Yehudah Leib Alter of Ger, translated by Rabbi David Shapiro, *Judaism* 12:2, Spring 1963

Page 69:   Servants? . . .   from *Wars of the Jews*, Book 7, Chapter 8, by Flavius Josephus, translated by William Whiston

Page 70:   When Israel left . . .   adapted from *The Psalms* by Rabbi Samson Raphael Hirsch

Page 70:   His domain . . .   ibid.
Page 70:   O sea . . .   ibid.
Page 71:   I am ready . . .   Rabbi Judah Loew ben Bezalel, Maharal of Prague
Page 71:   Rebuilding Jerusalem . . .   from *Israel: An Echo of Eternity* by Dr. Abraham Joshua Heschel

Page 71:   Rejoicing brings forth rejoicing . . . *Zohar, Raya Mehemna Bo,* 40b
Page 72:   The ritual . . .   from *Jewish Dietary Laws* by Rabbi Samuel H. Dresner

Page 74:   Matzah, Maror . . .   from *The Hasidic Anthology* by Rabbi Louis I. Newman

Page 77: Tzafun . . . Rabbi Yehudah Leib Alter of Ger, translated by Rabbi David Shapiro, *Judaism* 12:2, Spring 1963

Page 77: Yaḥatz . . . Rabbi Harold Schulweis

Page 79: Matzah and Morality . . . adapted from Rabbi Abraham Joshua Heschel of Apt, *The Hasidic Anthology* by Rabbi Louis I. Newman

Page 79: Let us praise Him . . . *Genesis Rabbah* 43:7

Page 80: Praised are You . . . *Berakhot* 48b

Page 80: Adonai who sustains all life . . . ibid.

Page 84: In a profound theological sense . . . from *Understanding Conservative Judaism* by Rabbi Robert Gordis

Page 85: Seven thousand killed . . . from *Wanderings* by Rabbi Chaim Potok

Page 86: He blessed our fathers . . . from *The Condition of Jewish Belief* by Rabbi David Greenberg

Page 86: Abraham, Isaac and Jacob . . . from *God in Search of Man* by Dr. Abraham Joshua Heschel

Page 87: There is neither eating nor drinking . . . *Berakhot* 17a

Page 90: We thank You for the land . . . adapted from *Passover Haggadah* by Rabbi Marcus Lehmann

Page 91: Holy city, holy land . . . Rabbi Naḥman of Bratzlav, as quoted in *In Time and Eternity* by Professor Nahum Glatzer

Page 93: I am ready . . . Rabbi Judah Loew ben Bezalel, Maharal of Prague

Page 95: In the Warsaw Ghetto . . . from *In Warshaver Ghetto iz Ḥodesh Nisan* by Bunim Heller

Page 95: The Jews of Bergen-Belsen . . . adapted from *The Language of Prayer* by Professor Nahum Glatzer

Page 97: I believe that a wondrous breed . . . Theodore Herzl as quoted in *The Zionist Idea* by Rabbi Arthur Hertzberg

Page 97: The land of Israel . . . Rabbi Abraham Isaac Kook, ibid.

Page 99: Ani ma'amin . . . from *The Tiger Beneath the Skin* by Zvi Kolitz

Page 101: Rabbi Naftali of Ropschitz . . . derived from Rabbi Harold Schulweis

Page 103: No hunger . . . *Mishneh Torah, Hilkhot Melakhim* 12:5 by Moses Maimonides

Page 105: The prophet Elijah . . . from *The Pharisees* by Rabbi Louis Finkelstein

Page 106: Each of us . . . *Mishneh Torah, Hilkhot Teshuvah* 5:1–4 by Moses Maimonides

Page 107: It is the object . . . *Moreh Nevukhim* 3:37 by Moses Maimonides

Page 107: When we enjoy . . . *Berakhot* 35 a–b

Page 108: Adonai listens . . . adapted from *The Origin and Meaning of Hasidism* by Professor Martin Buber

Page 108: Delivered from death? . . . from *A Beggar in Jerusalem* by Professor Elie Wiesel

Page 110: He answered by setting me free . . . Rabbi Louis Finkelstein, from *Passover Haggadah* edited by Maurice Samuel

Page 111: I shall not die . . . from *The Jewish Return into History* by Professor Emil L. Fackenheim

Page 112: Deliver us, Adonai . . . selections from I. Maccabees chapters 3–4

Page 113: I call heaven and earth . . . *Tanna de'vei Eliyahu* 48

Page 113: You are my God . . . from *Aspects of Rabbinic Theology* by Professor Solomon Schechter

Page 119: To Him praise is due . . . *Contra Apion*, Book 2, by Flavius Josephus translated by William Whiston

Page 119: To You, only to You . . . adapted from *Passover: Its History and Tradition* by Dr. Theodore Gaster

Page 120: The construction of the world . . . *Tanḥuma Kedoshim* 10

Page 121: Melodies, memories . . . from *The Rabbi of Bacharach* by Heinrich Heine

Page 122: Who knows three . . . adapted from *Legends of the Jews* by Professor Louis Ginzberg

Page 130: Just one kid . . . adapted from *Legends of the Jews* by Professor Louis Ginzberg

Page 132: Omer refers to the offering . . . Rabbi Jules Harlow

Page 133: Just as one who expects . . . *Moreh Nevukhim* 3:43 by Moses Maimonides

Page 135: I am ready . . . Rabbi Judah Loew ben Bezalel, Maharal of Prague

PERMISSIONS

We are grateful to the publishers and authors listed below for having granted us permission to print excerpts from the following works:

Wanderings by Chaim Potok, reprinted by permission of Alfred A. Knopf, Inc. © 1978

Jewish Dietary Laws by Samuel H. Dresner, reprinted by permission of Burning Bush Press © 1959

Amid These Storms by Winston Churchill, reprinted by permission of Charles Scribner's Sons © 1932, copyright renewed

The Zionist Idea by Arthur Hertzberg, reprinted by permission of Doubleday and Co. Inc. © 1959 Arthur Hertzberg

The Earth is the Lord's by Abraham Joshua Heschel © 1949 Abraham Joshua Heschel, copyright renewed © 1977 Sylvia Heschel, reprinted by permission of Farrar, Straus and Giroux, Inc.

God in Search of Man by Abraham Joshua Heschel, reprinted by permission of Farrar, Straus and Giroux, Inc. © 1956

Israel: An Echo of Eternity by Abraham Joshua Heschel © 1967, 1968, 1969 Abraham Joshua Heschel, reprinted by permission of Farrar, Straus and Giroux, Inc.

The Sabbath by Abraham Joshua Heschel, © 1951 Abraham Joshua Heschel, copyright renewed © 1979 Sylvia Heschel, reprinted by permission of Farrar, Straus and Giroux, Inc.

Passover Haggadah edited by Maurice Samuel, reprinted by permission of Hebrew Publishing Company © 1942

In Warshaver Ghetto iz Hodesh Nisan by Bunim Heller, reprinted by permission of the author

"Sons and Mystics" by Louis Jacobs, *The London Jewish Chronicle*, March 28, 1980, reprinted by permission of the author

The Pharisees by Louis Finkelstein, reprinted by permission of the Jewish Publication Society of America © 1960

"From the Classics" reprinted by permission of *Judaism* Magazine

The Tiger Beneath the Skin by Zvi Kolitz, Creative Age Press, reprinted by permission of the author © 1974

The Condition of Jewish Belief compiled by the Editors of *Commentary* Magazine © 1966 The American Jewish Committee, reprinted by permission of Macmillan Publishing, Inc.

American Judaism: Adventure in Modernity by Jacob Neusner, reprinted by permission of Prentice-Hall, Inc. © 1972

Understanding Conservative Judaism by Robert Gordis, **The** Rabbinical Assembly © 1978

A Beggar in Jerusalem by Elie Wiesel, translated by Lily Edelman, reprinted by permission of Random House, Inc. © 1970

Souls on Fire by Elie Wiesel, translated by Marion Wiesel, reprinted by permission of Random House © 1972

The Meaning of God in Modern Jewish Religion by Rabbi Mordecai Kaplan, reprinted by permission of The Reconstructionist Press © 1962

In Time and Eternity by Nahum Glatzer, reprinted by permission of Schocken Books, Inc. © 1961

The Hasidic Anthology by Louis I. Newman, reprinted by permission of Schocken Books, Inc. © 1963

The Jewish Return into History by Emil L. Fackenheim, reprinted by permission of Schocken Books, Inc. © 1978

The Rabbi of Bacharach by Heinrich Heine, translated by E. B. Ashton, reprinted by permission of Schocken Books, Inc. © 1947, copyright renewed © 1975

Aspects of Rabbinic Theology by Solomon Schechter, reprinted by permission of Schocken Books, Inc. © 1961

Tales of the Hasidim: Early Masters by Martin Buber, reprinted by permission of Schocken Books, Inc. © 1947

Pentateuch and Haftorahs by Dr. J.H. Hertz, reprinted by permission of Soncino Press, Ltd. © 1964

Festivals of the Jewish Year by Theodore H. Gaster, reprinted by permission of William Morrow and Co. © 1953